#90
18⁰⁰
‹ 4-18
RARE

5-07

TWENTY YEARS UNDER
THE SEA

"The Helmet Was Lifted and I Told My Story"

TWENTY YEARS UNDER THE SEA

By

J. E. WILLIAMSON

ILLUSTRATED

THE JUNIOR LITERARY GUILD
AND
HALE, CUSHMAN & FLINT
New York   *1936*

———————

PRINTED IN THE UNITED STATES OF AMERICA
BY THE POLYGRAPHIC COMPANY OF AMERICA, N.Y.

TO
ALONZO FOREST CATHEY
AND
THOMAS SOMERVILLE SOUTHGATE

CONTENTS

●

vii

ILLUSTRATIONS

●

XI

RELIEF MAP
OF THE
BAHAMA ISLANDS
and ADJACENT REGIONS

With particular reference to underseas
contours as shown by soundings

Figures indicate ocean depths in fathoms
1 fathom = 6 feet

With acknowledgement to
The American Museum of Natural History

```
0        50        100
STATUTE   MILES
```

2655

3070

DOR

2803

ACKLIN
I.

1758

Mariguana I.

2038

Grand
Caicos

1975

2939

1484

291

5

7

2871

1579

2059

7

12

17

GT. INAGUA
I.

ISLANDS

SANTO DOMINGO

HAITI

HAITI

TWENTY YEARS UNDER
THE SEA

INTRODUCTION

MY father's people came from Scotland and it was
here that he was born. John Williamson, his
father, was the youngest of nine brothers, all six-footers
and shipbuilders. John married Agnes Bell at Annan,
Scotland, and later they moved down to the sea and
ships at Liverpool, the saltiest of seaports, bringing
with them Charles, their tiniest infant, who was to
become my seafaring father.

On the day I was born my father was navigating his
ship under double reef topsails around the tip of Cape
Horn. Here near the bottom of the world and surrounded by mountainous seas, he was thousands of
miles away from home, yet only on the first leg of a
voyage. In those days months, even years, might pass
before a sailor could make his home port again. In fact
I was nearly three years old before my father cast his
seafaring eye on the trim of my rigging.

I remember hazily the day he breezed into our home
at Liverpool bringing with him the tang of the sea.
The house seemed crowded when he arrived. Everyone stood at attention. I don't think he more than
glanced at me for he carried in with him his latest
invention. I might be my mother's important new

infant, but he had brought home a baby of his own. No one had ever seen the like of it. It might have been a model for a perpetual motion machine. But, lo and behold, when he opened it up, it was a perfect folding baby carriage, a collapsible perambulator.

Then I began to travel, perambulated about the busy port. Whether the main purpose of this first trip conducted by my inventor father was to exhibit his offspring or his invention, it didn't matter. It was the beginning of wondrous days for me. Each time my father was home he would take me down to the docks where I could sniff delightedly at the spicy odours of strange cargoes and the smell of tar and ropes, gaze in awe and wonder at the stately sailing ships, their lofty spars crossed with great yard-arms, and hear the rattle and whine of tackle and the laughter of jolly sailors as they met along the water front.

But these excursion days were always short lived. My father had to be off to sea again. Our family life revolved about his sailings and the happy days when we could welcome him home again. Each time he returned he brought with him some new creation of his mind and hands.

One day he returned with an idea of great importance. There was a gathering of the clans at our home, and that night they repaired to the lawn where my father was to demonstrate his latest invention. The idea of it had come to him while sailing through the foggy banks of Newfoundland, eyes strained to avoid the fishing craft that bobbed about with winking red and green lights. These dancing gleams had been his inspiration and from them he had worked out a signal code.

Now with whispered prophecies and high hopes, the demonstration began, my father operating the controls. Red, green and white lights blinked through the darkness at the foot of the lawn, spelling out words. The messages were easily understood. It was a valuable invention and destined to be used the world over. There was much enthusiasm and my uncles wanted to finance the project and have it patented at once. But my father had other ideas and took the invention back to sea with him, probably to work on it and improve it.

Later, in New York, he took his model and the fully outlined plans for its development to the office of a patent agent, and requested him to get out a patent on the device. Then he went off to sea again. Many months later, upon his return to New York, he dashed up to the office where he had left his invention, but there was no sign of the man with whom he had left it. He had disappeared completely and some other business concern was occupying his quarters. No one knew anything about him. To add to the bewilderment of the inventor he picked up a scientific journal and was startled to read that someone in France had taken out a patent on the identical device he had submitted, alike in every detail to his. Then his fighting blood was aroused. He left his ship to search for the man who had perpetrated this crime, intent upon committing murder if he ever found the missing purveyor of patents whom he firmly believed had stolen his ideas.

However, before there were serious consequences, the inventor cooled down, and in the meantime had decided to live on shore. The next thing we learned was that he was building a hotel and a dam up in the mountains of Vermont. The project was nearing completion when my mother, sister, brother and myself left Liverpool for America.

We got to Vermont for a family reunion just the day before the opening of the hotel. It was then that I got my first real good look at the captain in action. I had heard of his great ability but was still a bit sceptical in my nine-year-old way of thinking. My mother had shown me newspaper notices concerning an enormous flagpole he had erected near the hotel. My father had searched the Vermont woods for its loftiest pine-tree. Farmers and natives had come from miles around to see how he would put this monster log upright in a hole. So I immediately checked up on this flagpole, and there it was upright, as straight as a die, towering high in the air, white and shining. And not only that, but on top of it was a topmast, almost as long as the flagpole itself. On the ground was the weather vane, filigreed out of brass and fully five feet long, a perfect reproduction of a mountain trout. When my father put this glittering fish in place at the top of the topmast, slid down the ropes true sailor fashion, and sent up the fluttering stars and stripes amid the cheers of the assembled throng, he made his first big hit with me.

The hotel project was a big success and my father's contract was up. He had been asked to run the hotel, but this was far too tame an occupation for him. Already he was longing again to be off and in a few days he was gone, heading south. He was soon in the business of ships again, this time at the seaports of Norfolk and Newport News, Virginia, twin Liverpools where the shipping of the world put in for trade. Combining his training in shipbuilding with his seafaring experience, my father was now in the business of fitting ships for grain and cattle. So my mother gathered up the trailing family and arrived at our new home in Virginia. "Carry Me Back to Old Virginny" had been my mother's favourite song in England. I remembered it as a lullaby, and here we were in the old Virginia of the song. My mother was busy again as a home-maker. If she had any extra talents she had no time to develop them, as her days were full in looking after my father, two sons and a daughter, already showing marked signs of being jibs off the old mainsail.

These were boom days in the business of grain and cattle shipping. Ships and more ships came trailing into the Virginia ports to carry out their bulging cargoes. Before the grain could be poured from the great elevators into the ships, the vessels must be prepared for it, first by dividing the holds into compartments with heavily-braced partitions. Then in the four corners of the between-decks wing feeders were built to feed grain into the lower holds as the cargo of grain settled when the ship laboured in the open sea. If this work of fitting was not well done, the grain would start moving, sometimes resulting in the tragic loss of the ship, which would turn completely over in a storm.

In fitting a ship for cattle the danger was not quite so serious, for the cattle were carried mainly on deck and in stalls. Those were trying times for the transfer of cattle. Often the entire load would be carried away in a gale, stalls, cattle and everything slipping off into the sea. When this happened it was time for them to go. The ship had reached the limit of its ability to hold such a deck load, and had to disgorge.

One day a queen of the sea came sailing into port like a great white butterfly with a hundred square wings. It was a full-rigged ship and painted pure white from stem to stern. To add to the excitement I found that the captain of the ship was an old sea friend of my father.

At our home at night I heard them recounting their glamorous days at sea. They told of the era of sailing ships—white wings that never grew weary—days when a man's credentials for supremacy on shipboard were held in his two horny fists, and to get to the top he had to be able to lick every man under him, and be ready at any time to prove that he could. I listened as they told of battling with the elements, marine and human, of gales and shipwrecks, of months at sea when death and disease walked the decks, of the strain of long voyages and mutiny. Their recollections ran the gamut from the heat of the tropics to the bitter cold of the regions of ice where these two as youngsters had leaned over the yard-arms and with long poles had beat the ice from the sails as the sleet and rain fell. I could imagine the cutting pain of the cold and the hardships endured as a matter of course by the hardy men of the sea.

Suddenly the captain of the great white ship nearly took my breath away when he asked my father if he would allow me to go to sea with him. He was bound for Spain with a full cargo of oak staves for the barrels used in the wineries there. I had watched for days while they had loaded these staves. The smell of the wood and the atmosphere of the ship with its fluttering white sails had held me entranced, and now to think of a voyage on this ship seemed almost too good to be true. It was an anxious moment for me as my father pondered the question of my going to sea. Then he smiled and thanked the captain for the offer. From that moment on I was getting ready to go, and fairly walking on air. Finally the loading of the ship was completed and the hatches were battened down. My clothes were now in a bundle as I prepared my good-bye speech, rehearsing it carefully so it would be short and sweet. And then, boy fashion, I began to be sorry about leaving home, but this was too big a chance to miss. I said good-bye to my mother with difficulty and went to my father who cut short my farewell remarks with a firm, final statement, "You're not going." And that was all there was to it. I was too crushed to say anything. All I could do was go down to the dock and watch my dream ship sail majestically out of the port. Leaning to the breeze its billowing sails were straining with the wind. Finally it faded from view as the scene was dimmed to my tear-filled eyes. I shall always remember that white-winged ship. Out through the Virginia capes it sailed to disappear for ever, with its gallant captain and crew. What happened to the ship no one ever knew. Somewhere out in the reaches of the ocean, the sea had swallowed it up.

To keep me from dreaming of deep sea voyages, my father kept me always at work. If I was not to go to sea, I was going to get the discipline of the sea, at home.

One day he told me to attend to a job connected with his barges, for he expected two ships in for fitting. I had every intention of carrying out his instructions to the letter, perhaps a bit later than he expected, but, lured by the thought of my shotgun and dog, off I went to the woods nearby. A few hours later I was back and had placed in the kitchen a pair of rabbits and a bird or so. I was breezily on my way through the house when I came to a screen door between two of the rooms. I had just reached for the knob when directly on the other side of the screen I saw the immobile figure of my father. He was dressed for the street, immaculate and sartorially correct in pin-striped trousers and with a senatorial cutaway draping his enormous chest.

His question and my answer were quickly exchanged. Nothing unusual might have happened, had I not accompanied my reply with a misplaced grin. Then something shot out toward my head. I saw stars, lots of 'em. Had I been kicked by a mule? I was spinning across the room. Now my vision was clearing. I was down on the floor. I could see my father still standing behind the door, though a hole in the screen marked the spot where his ponderous fist had shot through. There was no great harm done except to the door, and we both made our exits in opposite directions. Later, bucksaw in hand, I was busy in the woodshed when my father's hand was laid on my shoulder with, "I'm sorry, my son." I had nothing to say. It was the first time in my life that he had ever struck or hurt me. I took the apology with the blow.

So I fell in with his rule always to keep busy with at least two jobs awaiting in the offing. At night I received training in music and a home course in engineering.

In addition to these studies, I also graduated from high school.

During all free hours I had plenty of work to do in the hectic enterprise of ship fitting. Work on several ships at once meant day and night labour, as the ships were held up in the meantime. There could be no let-up in our work and the excitement of it reached into the home. There was no such thing as a regular time for meals. There were comings and goings and eating at all hours. However, I learned one thing against my father's wishes, and that was occasionally to go on working for forty-eight hours at a stretch. If he caught me at it he sent me home, or thought he did, for I would go to some other ship and get to work again.

This was excitement to my liking. Men working and shouting on the decks and in the holds of the ships. Often an avalanche of grain would come pouring in before we had finished the wing feeders in the between-decks, and that meant the thrill of desperate work to finish and get out of the holds, sweat pouring from us, and every man wearing a large damp sponge tied over his mouth with a bandana handkerchief to help him breathe in the heavy dust. But there was the sport of it, the race to finish, to complete the one job and go on to the next. To me it was a thrill to be in the maze of ships' holds and the traffic of the docks. If the old man wanted work, I would give it to him and like it.

When I was sixteen years old it was decided that I should enter the big shipyards at Newport News. I was duly entered as apprentice in the department of marine draughtsmen. Here I could learn everything I did not already know about ships. Get acquainted with every rivet and gadget from truck to keel, of battleships, cruisers and torpedo boats and every other sort of a ship right down through the line to the sea-roving tramp.

Up to this time drawing was as simple to me as breathing. I had walked through all of it in my school work with ease, for I had learned to think in terms of pictures. I found it much the easiest way. Yet the stern formality of the drafting board and the tedious details of this new work did not represent as free and un-trammelled an art as I would have wished, but I dug· into it, nevertheless. Later when my period for work in the yards came around, and I was sent to the great steel hulls, I began to get restless, for in the meantime I had visited machine shops, pattern shops, moulding lofts, the foundries and seen great castings made. I had been to these places where the draughtsmen's blue prints were carefully read and made to come true. The one thing that took my eye and caught my fancy was pattern making—the art of creating in wood from the blue print, everything from ship's engines to propeller blades, all later to be cast in iron, brass and steel. That was just to my liking. If I could get into

25

this kind of work it would be the next thing to heaven, so I begged for a transfer and completed my five years' course at the shipyard in the pattern making department.

Then I decided to strike out for myself. The lure of the west was calling me, and I answered. My adventures that followed included a burnt cork era in this wild oats period. I toured as an end man with a minstrel show. On top of my black-face experience I made an important decision. I would be a newspaper man—a cartoonist on a big city newspaper. And of all the things I had decided to do this was the toughest of all to accomplish.

My first step was to enter Reed's School of Art in Denver, Colorado. The first night I reported for study at the school, I found myself in the company of about two dozen young men and girls, in the ante-room preparing for class. They wanted to know if I had paper. I said "No," and they supplied me with some. They also fixed me up with charcoal and other supplies and a smock which made me feel quite the artist. In the easel-filled drawing hall we prepared to sketch. Out came a model, in the nude, and the drawing commenced. I was more interested in the model than the drawing. The room was chilly and so was the model who, during the rest periods, would step down from the platform and poke up the fire in the stove. After a half-hour of sketching I had outlined my study when Reed, the master, came in. When he got around to me on his tour of inspection he gave me a quizzical look, but taking my charcoal he showed me how to throw in the shadows of my drawing more boldly, and asked me to see him afterwards. I had made a glaring error in coming to the life class, commencing at the top of the ladder, when I should have come in on a night when they were working on still life studies and started in at the bottom. Accordingly I entered the still life class, but in a few weeks I had mopped up everything and got back into the life class, much to the consternation of two girl artists who had been trying for a year or more to get out of still life. I liked this art business, and I enjoyed the wonder city I was living in, a mile above the sea, but at last I succumbed to the lure of the sea level and the smell of the salt sea marshes. So one day I folded up my kit and carried it back to old Virginia.

I was back east now and looking for a newspaper job. One day I cartooned a seven-act Keith vaudeville show and took the pictures to a local paper. The next day I was on the staff. I had plenty of ideas, but to perfect my treatment—master all the tricks of the pen and brush, for I was determined to be as good as the best—proved a rocky road to travel. It carried me on explorations through every department of a newspaper. I studied engraving with its wet plates, line cuts, half tones and colour reproductions all the way from Norfolk to Boston, and back again. I also did some reporting and worked for a year on one paper as staff photographer, attending art school when possible. The routine was easy but reaching the high point of perfection was not. The only remedy I knew was to put in heartless hours. Twenty hours a day was the usual thing, but it was just to my liking. There was little talking to be done, just sketching, drawing, photographing and writing. The rush and clatter of newspaper offices gradually became home to me. Often when through for the day I figured that the few hours for sleep might just as well be spent at the office, and would wake up with my feet under the drawing board. If trying hard would bring perfection, I was slowly, if not surely, on my way somewhere in that direction when my story opens.

Chapter I

THE FIRST PICTURES OUT OF THE DEPTHS

A NEWSPAPER man on the hunt for news might best describe my state of being as I stepped, one day, into a magic world that later became a reality. It happened in the old seaport of Norfolk, Virginia. I had strolled down a narrow street with the sea and ships at its end. Long, mysterious shadows filled the space between the ancient buildings looming ghostly and unreal against the glow of the setting sun. Silence reigned. The place seemed utterly deserted and forgotten. Above the crooked roofs and sagging chimneys was a fathomless green sky, and a strange sensation of standing on the bottom of the sea among the ruins of some sunken city came to me. I knew it was visionary, but I had always been fascinated by the legend of the lost Atlantis, and by the tales of known sunken cities of Yucatan and the submerged Port Royal in Jamaica.

Standing there in the weird half-light of a dying day, I visualized these cities once peopled by humans and now the haunts of creatures of the sea. What wondrous stories they held! What astounding pictures they would present if photographed! Perhaps there would be wrecked ships, loaded treasure galleons, rotting in the silence of the once busy streets. I was seized with a sudden inspiration to make photographs of the world beneath the sea: that it had never been done, made the idea more alluring. It would be a real "scoop" for my paper, it would be a real adventure, as thrilling and exciting as the exploration of some unknown land. Fired with eagerness, the difficulties to be overcome never occurred to me at the time.

In the life of a newspaper man, the guiding star—the lure that keeps him ever at his task—is the hope that he will come upon the one big story that will surpass all other adventures in his years of search for news. I believed I had the idea that was to produce that story. All regular assignments were forgotten. What were mere local colour and ordinary events compared to the mysterious happenings in the new strange world hidden from human eyes by the restless sea?—a world peopled by strange monsters, by creatures bizarre, utterly incredible and undreamed of. Always I had loved the sea. I had been born with the sea in my blood, inherited from seafaring ancestors. All my life I had lived near the sea, and always I had been filled with a curiosity, a longing to know what lay beneath its enigmatic surface.

Now, with my mind crowded with the visionary scheme of taking pictures beneath the sea, my training in mechanics came to my aid. Yet I might never have achieved my goal, or even thought of the idea, had it not been for an invention which my father, Captain Charles Williamson, after a lifetime of seafaring, had devised. He was just perfecting his marvellous deep-sea salvaging device, a flexible metal tube capable of reaching great depths. The tube made easy access to the sea floor, and thick green-glass ports allowed the occupant of the work chamber at the bottom a somewhat restricted view of undersea surroundings, enabling him to direct and operate giant grapples and arms when working on sunken wrecks. Herein lay the solution of my problem. The small observation chamber would have to be enlarged and equipped with clear-glass windows. There would also have to be banks of powerful electric lights to illuminate the depths beyond the reach of sunlight. I was confident that with these additions and alterations photographs of the ocean's floor and of the denizens of the deep would be possible. First, however, I would have to persuade my father to lend me his invention and allow me to alter it to suit my requirements. I thought this would be no easy matter, for he was tuning up his apparatus in preparation for tests to be conducted by the United States Government, and my scheme would, I felt, appear to him as of little value or importance. However, I found that I had underrated my father's vision and his interest in my experiment. While in lending me his invention I am

sure he felt very much like a mother who gives over her only child for a dangerous surgical operation, yet he agreed to let me go ahead. As a final act of confidence and co-operation, he piloted the outfit down the Elizabeth River and, at the opening of Chesapeake Bay, turned over to me his precious boats and undersea equipment.

But all was not easy sailing. I had a regular job and the big story perforce must wait on the more prosaic but necessary tasks assigned by the *Virginian Pilot*, the morning newspaper of Norfolk, on whose staff I was photographer, artist, and often reporter to boot. Along with these duties, weeks of ceaseless work and experiment followed. From dawn until dark I laboured. I lay awake at night striving to solve problems that seemed insurmountable. Changes, alterations, and adjustments followed in endless succession. At last the day came when my experiments were to end. I descended in the tube, and, crouched in my photographic chamber, spent the afternoon "at home" with the fishes thirty feet below the surface of the bay. Outside streaming banners of clear light pierced to the floor of the bay. Clumps of seaweed were revealed, swaying in the current, while in the dim, pale green distance bloomed inscrutable shadows, hinting of mysteries farther on. All about my chamber, undisturbed by the strange invader of their realm, the fishes swam lazily through the green sea water or stopped

"The tube made easy access to the sea floor"
THE WILLIAMSON SUBMARINE TUBE IN OPERATION

to peer curiously into the glass of my window. Over and over again, I focussed my camera and pressed the shutter, filled with tense excitement, nerves a-tingle. Would my experiment be a success? Would the plates actually record the scene before me, or should I find that all my hopes, my weeks of work had been for nothing?

I shall never forget the anxiety and suspense that attended the development of those first plates exposed beneath the sea. With bated breath I watched the silver emulsion darkening under the action of the chemicals in the little red light of my dark room, and I shall never forget the thrill of elation that swept over me when, little by little, the outline of the fishes appeared. Finally, the whole scene stood out clearly in all its pristine beauty. I had succeeded! I had actually taken photographs beneath the sea. Best of all, I had made snapshots. Instantly I realized the tremendous importance of this achievement. If undersea photographs could be made at the speed I had used, then motion pictures could be made under similar conditions. "Movies" meant magic even in 1913, when the industry was yet in its infancy and had not yet learned to talk.

I didn't sleep much that night. I was too busy planning the future and too anxious to get to my editor and spring the news on him how motion pictures could be made under the sea. I wanted to submit to him my

plans for an expedition to the clear waters of the West Indies.

The next day I placed the photographs and the data upon his desk, and stepped back to watch him pore over the details and grow into a strange mood of enthusiasm, confirming my growing convictions. Finally he exploded, "Great, Williamson, you've got something!" In one hand he held my few small photographs, the like of which had never been seen before, and with a bang his other hand descended upon the pile of drawings and plans for my proposed expedition to the floor of the ocean in the West Indies. "We'll have a full page on this for Sunday," continued the editor. "Rush your lay-out and I'll write the story myself. This is news! Do you realize you have made the first real undersea photographs in history? No one has ever gone beneath the sea with a camera and brought back a successful photograph of life in the depths."

The first account of my undersea photography published in the *Virginian Pilot* aroused unbounded interest throughout the world. Pictures actually taken at the bottom of the sea seemed amazing, yet looking back on them now, those first submarine photographs appear woefully crude and inadequate. It was the feat rather than the pictures that counted, for I had actually accomplished the seemingly impossible: I had photographed life on the floor of the ocean, and proved, to my own satisfaction at least, that motion pictures could be taken under the sea.

Though the *Pilot* might have backed my proposed expedition, it never had the opportunity of doing so. Hundreds of letters and telegrams from metropolitan magazines and newspapers came in a flood as a result of that first account of successful under-ocean photography. Among them was a telegram inviting me to come to New York and exhibit my pictures at the First International Motion Picture Exposition, which was about to open at the Grand Central Palace. With my half-dozen four by five negatives, a few prints, and the papers with my plans in my pockets, I hurried to New York to accept the invitation.

The *Pilot's* story had altered my life completely. I actually was in the movies and didn't know it!

Oddly enough, I was not a professional photographer. Strictly speaking, I was a marine engineer, having taken a five-year course in that profession. For the past four years, however, I had been on the staff of several newspapers, including the *Philadelphia Record* where my sport cartoons had become a popular feature. But photography had always appealed to me, and when I resigned from the *Record* to accept a position on the *Virginian Pilot* it was a first stepping stone on the road toward a life work of which I had never dreamed!

In Manhattan I was met with enthusiastic greetings at the Exposition, and was allotted a booth for my pictures. Then, "Where is your exhibit?" inquired the manager. I drew the package of pictures and negatives out of my hip pocket. Not a very impressive exhibit nor one that seemed destined to fill a good-sized booth, but I assured the manager that I would increase its size before the show opened on Monday. I hurried away to obtain enlargements of the pictures. However, I had forgotten that it was Saturday, that business ended at noon, and that photographers had locked their doors and departed for their holiday that hot week-end. Vainly I tried every studio from Forty-sixth Street to Herald Square, when I chanced upon the Rembrandt Studios, where a friendly German and his wife proved Good Samaritans and came gallantly to my rescue.

Among the enlargements made was one six feet wide, coloured with a sponge, which crowned the pictorial display that filled my booth at the opening of the Exposition. The picture of that patch of sea bottom with its fishes, just a few square yards of the vast ocean's floor, proved one of the greatest attractions of the show.

A hectic week followed. Thousands of persons—professors, movie stars, financiers, producers, photographers of still and motion pictures, cinema exhibitors, and the general public—crowded about the booth from opening to closing time. The visitors' book was filled with signed expressions of praise and congratulations from famous men and women. Among the autographs was that of John Bunny of hallowed memory. This comedian and his elongated companion, Flora Finch, were the romantic film fun makers of the period. At that time the "Birth of a Nation" had not yet been produced, but with the growing interest of the public there was no doubt about the movies being a money-making business. So I was riding in with the pioneer movie makers. I had discovered something new for the camera, a virgin field for entertainment and profit —submarine moving pictures. Offers of financial aid came freely and unsolicited.

Money was all-important. An expedition to the West Indies to invade Neptune's realm with a camera would be costly; and I realized that only in the crystal clear waters of the tropics would it be possible to attain the results at which I aimed. Until I had conferred with my brother George, who had taken a deep interest in my experiments, I was not sure whether I wanted the enterprise financed by outside capital, or whether it would be better to organize a company at home. Prominent bankers and business men of Norfolk had expressed interest in the scheme, and after discussing the matter from every angle, we decided to decline with thanks the offers of extensive promotion from the north, and accept the more conservative support of our friends in the south. A company was formed and ample funds seemed assured to carry out the undersea motion picture expedition to the West Indies. After all,

39

we should pay no fabulous salaries to movie stars, we should receive no bills for wardrobes, though our actors from the finny tribe might wear the most gorgeous and glittering costumes.

This expedition was to be the big test, the real proof of the future possibilities of submarine photography. Many anxious days and nights were devoted to planning everything to the most minute detail. I visited the Pennsylvania steel mills and arranged for the casting of my new deep-sea "photosphere," which, complete with its great glass windows, would weigh nearly four tons. Optical experts in Rochester accepted my specifications for lenses and film. Mercury vapour lighting engineers contracted to provide proper illumination by means of my new deep sea lamps. Everything appeared to be moving smoothly, and I saw success ahead, when I was met in New York by one of my principal backers who informed me he had talked the matter over with his associates and that they had decided the whole scheme was too much of an experiment to warrant the necessary investment, and unless—— He didn't need to say any more. My next duty was to restore his confidence. He was a man whose opinion commanded respect in business matters, and no doubt he felt he was right. I had to admit that the margin of complete financial success was slim, and that we were investing with hopes, but with no certainty of profit. It was an undertaking never before

"Which would weigh nearly four tons"
THE PHOTOSPHERE DESIGNED BY THE AUTHOR

attempted. We were pioneers in every sense of the word. While I was confident of success myself, it was another matter to convince a very practical business man. I pointed out that my Chesapeake Bay experiments proved I could secure under-water photographs showing a radius of eight feet and confirmed the simple theory that I could photograph anything I could see, even through water. I could take pictures at far greater distances in the clear waters of the West Indies where the visibility was good for hundreds of feet. Moreover, in such waters, a motion picture camera could film successfully wonders hitherto unknown. However, my good friend remained unconvinced, until by chance I mentioned the name of an authority in the film business, who was anxious to support my project. A meeting was arranged between this man and the financier. As a result of this conference, my newly-formed company made over a fifty per cent interest to the optimistic film magnate in exchange for a motion picture camera, a camera man, the necessary film, and the promise to market the completed film to the best advantage.

With all equipment ready for shipment, and all business details arranged, I sailed for a voyage of reconnaisance to the port of Nassau in February of 1914. A blizzard swallowed the harbour of Norfolk as I steamed away toward the heaving seas in the Atlantic. After a stormy day, a summer-time feeling announced the warm waters of the Gulf Stream, that flowing sea of cobalt blue. There followed balmy days and starlit nights. At last one daybreak brought us to a tiny lighthouse. We had arrived at the bar off Nassau, main port of the Bahamas.

A shower of tropical sunshine descended as the tender entered the harbour, and I blinked with amazement at the transparency of the water. The sea was as clear as crystal.

"That's it!" I shouted involuntarily, to assure myself that it was true. If anyone heard me, he could not know of the months of anxiety behind my expression of joy. I was nearing my goal. I had arrived in a smiling land of wonders. Bright sunlight shimmered on the hillside city. Old forts gnarled the hill-tops on either side, and in between, the quaint buildings, pink and white, were like cameos, matted in flowers and palm-trees.

At masthead over the landing-place fluttered the Union Jack, a reminder of the far-flung British Empire. Picturesque sailing ships from the seven seas were cradled in the harbour. In this haven, in days gone by, pirates and smugglers had hatched out their schemes. Isolated, the place was self-contained with its ship-yards, ship chandlers, and sailors ever ready for adventure. Here I could find men and material for anything dealing with the sea.

After a month in Nassau, my work vessel was ready

43

to receive the many tons of equipment arriving and being unloaded under the watchful eye of my brother. From the first the brothers Williamson had been men of mystery to the islanders and, now, as they watched us transferring strange steel objects and queer-looking gear to an odd-looking craft with a huge hole in its bottom, they obviously considered us quite mad. At length our mystery ship swallowed the last of its load and was moved to anchorage in the back stream. Rapidly the apparatus was assembled. The massive undersea chamber slipped downward through the well into the sea with fifteen fathoms of the great flexible steel tube ready to be fixed into place. Then, with the one hundred and one connections made, the wiring for the undersea lamps was completed and we were ready for out submarine adventure.

No, not quite ready, for I was still awaiting the arrival of the next fortnightly steamer which would bring two additional members of the expedition. One was Carl L. Gregory, expert cameraman, who was blessed with an accumulation of motion picture knowledge. The other was Keville Glennan, now historian of the expedition and none other than the erstwhile editor of the *Virginian Pilot*. Declaring that, as he had covered my first big scoop and had, figuratively speaking, put me on the map, he was entitled to be in on the second—or at my finish.

My brother George, Gregory, Glennan, and myself

formed a likely quartet, the four undersea horsemen, destined to ride with the expedition to success or—but only a fleeting thought was ever given to the possibility of failure.

Chapter II

BENEATH TROPIC SEAS

NOW that everything—men and machinery—was in readiness, Nature suddenly conspired against us. For twelve days, black squalls, whipping winds and tumultuous seas held us, impotent prisoners, within the shelter of the coral reefs against which the great seas roared and pounded, flinging spray high in the air as in a fury at our temerity in attempting to learn the secrets of their depths.

With nothing else to do, we had time to give serious thought to what was before us. We discussed the relative chances of success or failure and jokingly I suggested that in case we failed, it might be advisable to vanish into the interior of the island.

At last the elements wearied of their futile rage and a glorious day dawned, with sparkling sunshine, scarcely a breeze and a perfect sun.

To an onlooker our vessel would have appeared idle, purposeless, almost deserted. But inside and below decks she was a hive of loosened energy, a tumult of joyous shouting, noisy work and feverish activity. With a whirr of gears, our tunnel of steel slid gently

46

into the sea. Like a mammoth antenna, the flexible
tube felt its way giving and taking to the currents,
curving to their flow, until five fathoms of its length
had been lowered through the open well in the bottom
of our craft. The chamber was close to the bottom.
The hour of our supreme test had arrived.

With a shout of elation I descended into the tube,
followed by the others. Reaching the photosphere I
stood spellbound at the sight which greeted me.
Could this be real, or was I dreaming? Nothing I
had ever imagined had equalled this. It was more than
I had ever dared hope for. Down from above through
the crystal clear waters streamed the bright sunlight,
which, striking the white marl bottom, was reflected
in a glittering, rippling plane of light. No artificial
illumination was needed. We couldn't fail in this light.
The camera would tell the story!

For our test we had several skilful diving boys already
enrolled as members of our crew. Shillings and quarter-
dollars were piled on deck and eagerly the black boys
pressed forward listening to my instructions. All was
ready. The boys were chattering like monkeys in the
excitement—not only were they to earn good "hard"
money by diving, but they were to be stars in the first
movie ever filmed under the sea. Descending into the
camera chamber where the movie apparatus was loaded
and focussed I gave the signal. "Go!" What a striking
study their muscular black bodies would make in

47

contrast to the light flooded stage set for them! What a great "shot" their struggles would make as they snatched for the elusive silver.

The camera was humming in action. A few fleeting shadows danced over the bottom of the sea. Nothing more. Where were the boys? Surely they must be down there somewhere. Why could I not see them? Had they failed us, or was there some optical illusion, some obtuse trickery in the undersea panorama before me? The explanation proved simple enough. The answer to the mystery was the big secret of the diving boys' trade. We had expected the coins to sink swiftly to the bottom, but instead, they moved slowly, aquaplaning, rocking and sliding through the water, easy money indeed for the wise young rascals who seized the flashing bits of silver before they were half-way down. It was a huge joke on us, but we soon fixed that by giving the coins a handicap and forcing the boys to wait until the silver was nearing the bottom before diving after it. This time there was no mystery, no puzzle. Down through the water dropped the coins, slowly, gently, catching the glint of the sun first on one side and then on the other as they descended. And down after them came the boys, flashing downward with long swift strokes, white-soled feet kicking, and leaving a trail of silvery bubbles in their wake. And what action! Before the windows of our photosphere, under the eye of the clicking camera, they fought and

48

struggled. They searched in the soft white marl for lost coins and looked like blue ghosts in the cloud of white ooze stirred up by their efforts. Again and again they dived into our field of vision, until the supply of coins was exhausted. But it was enough. We had shot the first motion pictures ever taken under the sea. I was supremely, crazily happy, for I was as certain as I had ever been of anything that the film had recorded every detail, that motion pictures beneath the sea were not only possible, but an accomplished fact. There was yet another test to be made. I must prove that my lights would enable me to take pictures at night when there was no natural illumination under the water. It would never have satisfied me to confine underseas movies to shoal water. I was blazing a trail to the darkest depths of the ocean.

That night the worst fears of the inhabitants of the island must have seemed confirmed. All day they had watched us from a safe distance. Now, in the darkness of night, a great circular arc of white appeared upon the black expanse of sea, with our vessel silhouetted like a tiny black island in its centre. That settled it. We were worse than crazy. We were working some sort of dark magic. Obeah! They were not far wrong, for as I flashed on my banks of lights in the submarine chamber the result seemed magical indeed. Terrified fish darted like wraiths from the blinding glare, only to return fascinated, curious to investigate this strange phenomenon. Upon the floor of the sea, creeping and crawling creatures were moving, attracted by the unwonted light. Everywhere, claws, horns and antennae stirred among the corals and marine life. In one spot the craning head and neck of a turtle stood stiffly erect, staring toward us with unwinking eyes. I jumped to the camera, and as it hummed into action suddenly all outside the chamber was commotion. A phosphorescent body shot into the lighted space and pounced on the turtle. Not for several moments did I recognize it as one of our diving boys, who, seeing the turtle revealed by our undersea illumination had promptly secured it for a feast.

We had pitched our dark-room in an old stone building buried in a cluster of coco-nut trees and fragrant flowers that opened at night. The darker the night the darker the room inside, for through chinks in the crumbling building could be seen the twinkling heavens above; here in this ancient structure haunted by ghosts of a romantic past, we would know our future. I helped with the ice and brought water from an aged well. My mind was in a jumble, and I felt like a prisoner who awaits the verdict of the jury. I kept as close as possible to the tanks and to the dark-room. Dead silence. Then grunts in the tank-room gave way to sounds which were more encouraging. I knew when the singing commenced it was time to go in, and I stole through the curtained opening with that wonderful feeling of exhilaration that comes from knowing that a victory has been won. It was there in that strip of film! In the tiny frames no larger than a row of postage stamps were the negatives. The first undersea motion pictures in the world! Best of all, the films exposed by our artificial light were fully as successful as those taken by sunlight.

The supreme moment, the successful climax of those weary months of effort, those countless obstacles and bitter disappointments, of nerve-racking days and sleepless nights, of endless plans and experiments had come on the stroke of midnight. Too excited to sleep, too filled with emotion to dream of retiring, I wandered to the edge of the sea that stretched black and mysterious, reflecting like a mirror the brilliant stars of the tropical sky above.

Not until the eastern sky paled with the coming of dawn did I seek our sleeping quarters where my three companions were snoring lustily. Yet judging by the pile of letters stamped and ready for the morning post, they too had been occupied with other matters than slumber since that epochal midnight hour. Within a week, parents, sweethearts and friends would all learn of the successful culmination of our endeavours, and I added my quota to His Majesty's mails by writing a full report of our triumph to our financiers, enclosing with it a section of the first underseas film.

The following week was one of hectic work, suc-

FROM ONE OF WILLIAMSON'S EARLY UNDERSEA FILMS—
THE HEROINE VISITS THE WRECK OF A SHIP

cesses and failures, experiments and surprises, high adventure and near tragedy. We had many prominent visitors, also. Buoyantly confident, now that our first tests had proved so successful, we rushed blindly ahead and sailed forth into the open sea. Deeper and deeper we lowered the photosphere at the end of its flexible tube. But we were veritable tenderfeet at this game. We were in an unknown realm dealing with strange forces and we had much to learn. We discovered this one day when we lowered our apparatus among the great coral reefs. Breathless with wonder at the weird beauty of the undersea life unfolding in colourful panorama before us, we were gazing entranced when, like a flock of frightened birds, a school of fish dashed past our window. The next instant the great steel photosphere tipped and swayed as we were caught in an underseas current. With a sickening, terrifying crash we were dashed against a great dome-shaped mass of coral. The flexible tube bent and, together with every-thing movable, we were tumbled head over heels. Yet in the terror and excitement of that moment my mind fastened upon one vital thing—the big glass window! If that went, if it were broken or even cracked, my experiments under the ocean would be over.

Fate was kind to us. By pure luck, or through the intervention of Providence, the glass did not strike the coral and the next moment we had dragged over the reef and once more were poised upright and safe in open water beyond the dangerous mass. The ingenious bending of the tube had saved us. Here was lesson number one. The depths of the sea were not so tranquil and calm as we had imagined. There were treacherous tides and currents below, as well as at the surface. Even when we rested apparently motionless in still water, the great steel tube bent in a long curve between our chamber and the vessel above. It behoved us to be mighty careful in future and to learn to navigate the depths and to avoid underseas reefs as skilfully as the mariner pilots his ship through channels on the surface.

During the next few hours we should have to be doubly careful, for His Excellency, the Governor of the Bahamas, was to pay us a visit, and with his own eyes gaze for the first time on the wonders of his under-water regions.

News of our success had spread rapidly. Our first visitor had been the local United States consul, who, after descending into the chamber and watching us work had written an official report to the State Department at Washington on our "alluring and commendable enterprise." "I actually descended far under water and so have actual knowledge of the application of the Williamson inventions to motion picture photography," he wrote. "The photographer sits in the work chamber with an ordinary camera securing motion picture material during many hours at a stretch." A very dry

and matter of fact description perhaps, but serving as proof to a sceptical world that we had succeeded.

Even the natives had altered their opinions of our sanity and purpose, and when the Governor and his wife and party boarded our launch for a trip beneath the sea, the natives regarded us with profound respect.

Seated in the photosphere behind the great glass window the Governor and his wife gazed entranced upon his "kingdom down under the sea." Ever expanding as we moved along was the jungle of waving, feathery plant-like gorgonias—sea feathers and sea fans, red, brown, black, mauve, golden and green. Then the jungle gave way to a forest of spreading coral trees with gorgeous fishes, like bright-plumaged tropical birds, flitting among the branches. A school of hunted fish swept by, flashing like jewels, their pursuer, a silvery menace, hard on their trail. An angelfish moved with languid grace through a shadowy grotto, while just below our window, a great wolf-fanged barracuda kept grim watch over a deep hole in the sea bed wherein he had bottled up his prey.

When our distinguished visitors had left, wilted collars and ties were cast aside, and, like bees in clover, we plunged to our neglected work.

Both day and night work was the order. Even the historian of the expedition abandoned his typewriter, rolled up his sleeves and went to work. Then, as the culmination of that week of labour, my brother, clad

'Perhaps . . . the remains of some old ship of Spain'
N DAVY JONES'S LOCKER

in a diving suit, dropped to the sea's floor among the coral reefs where we had discovered the wreck of some long-forgotten ship. In ghostly pantomime he moved about the ribs and backbone of the ancient hulk, while a stream of air bubbles rushed from the helmet to the surface far above. Here was a thrill! Many a treasure-laden galleon had been sunk in these seas. Among the rotted timbers the outlines of corroded cannon could be seen. Perhaps, unwittingly, we had come upon the remains of some high-pooped, pot-bellied old ship of Spain with a fortune in golden ingots and pieces of eight hidden in the tangle of sea growths within her hold. Our diver had caught the fever of adventure, the excitement of treasure seeking, and presently, poking about amid the wreckage he found the highly ornate brass bell of the old ship. And though no bars or bullion or silver coins rewarded his search, yet we obtained our treasure—treasure more precious to us than doubloons and plate—the recorded film of an actual treasure hunt at the bottom of the sea.

Our photography was perfect. For the entire week we had only the best of luck. We were impatient to let the people at home hear of our phenomenal success. The mails were far too slow for such important news and recklessly we cabled, caring not a snap of our fingers for expense, so intoxicated were we with victory.

Nevertheless, expense was a mighty serious matter.

For the first time I began to give the matter earnest consideration. The costs of the expedition were piling up with alarming rapidity. With a month or more before us, the question was how could we use time and money to the best advantage? A conference was called, and ways and means were discussed. The review was encouraging. Gala days were near—Empire Day and the King's Birthday—big celebrations in the loyal British Colony. We could take movies of life above as well as beneath the sea. Then in our undersea rendezvous were the game fish, tarpon and swordfish, the hunting preserves of shark and devil fish. No telling what was in store for us and our faithful camera.

Then came news of two scientific expeditions in neighbouring seas. Some of the greatest oceanographers from the Carnegie Institute and the Brooklyn Museum were in charge of the work. Here was a real opportunity. Near at hand were men of science who had probed the ocean to its greatest depth. They knew the undersea creatures by name and could classify them root and branch. Our knowledge of marine zoology was nil, but we had acquired a fund of practical knowledge regarding the private lives and habits of the creatures of the sea, so we invited the scientists to come down and have a look at their specimens in their native haunts.

Never shall I forget their enthusiasm as they gazed through our window upon the floor of the sea, which, for years, they had been studying and exploring quite blindly from the surface. Their visit opened up a new and undreamed-of field for the undersea camera—the photographic records of submarine life for the benefit of science. Here indeed lay unlimited possibilities. At any moment the searching eye of our camera might discover and record something entirely new in marine life. And presently it happened!

The leader of the Brooklyn Museum expedition was with me in the photosphere studying a school of parrot-fish and a hundred other species of tropical beauties when suddenly a strange creature appeared. Into our range of vision swam a weird, ugly fish two feet or more in length. Above its caricature of a face rose a staff and from the tip of this staff streamed a pure white flag! But, obviously, it was no flag of truce, or at least it was not recognized as such, for with one hurried glance at the monstrosity every fish in sight turned and dashed away as if for dear life. Alone, monarch of all he surveyed, the flag-carrier moved uncertainly in a circle, and then vanished in pursuit of the retreating fish.

We were to find out, however, that the bizarre and unannounced visitor was extremely rare, but not entirely unknown to science. Zoologists identified our photographs of the monster as a fish known to them by the Latin name of "Equus Punctatus," or "spotted horse." Though Spotted Horse would have found little favour as food for the stomach, it certainly provided much food for thought on the part of the scientists, for our specimen was a decided puzzle to them. Scientific descriptions of "Equus Punctatus" called for a single dorsal fin, while our photographs showed the fish to have two. Finally, the scientists concluded that some marauder must have bitten a section out of the dorsal adornment of our unorthodox creature, and let it go at that. But the upright staff with its white flag was not so readily disposed of. No "Spotted Horse" ever known had hoisted a flag. They shook their learned heads. There could be no mistake on our part. Photographs, like figures, do not lie. Finally they gave it up, after suggesting that the flagstaff was an abnormal growth, or some parasite clinging to our fish. No doubt they were correct, but abnormal or not, weird, ugly old Spotted Horse, flag and all, was a welcome addition to our "rogues' gallery" of fishes.

Chapter III

A DUEL WITH A MAN-EATER

BEFORE starting on the expedition, I had, in an optimistic moment, assured our financial backers that our undersea movies would include a shark fight —an actual combat between a man and a savage tiger of the sea. I had not for a moment forgotten that promise. In fact, I was constantly reminded of it as sharks flirted about our undersea chamber day and night. Just how the battle was to be staged was a problem I had not been able to solve. Then I received a letter reminding me of my confident assurance of a shark fight. This letter was like a long finger, pointing to the dramatic climax of our achievements. My promise must be made good, for time was getting short, funds were running low and the sharks were ready for business even if we were not.

Obviously the contest must be of short duration. Obviously, also, it must be fought directly in front of the camera which covered but twenty degrees of the circular arena outside my photosphere. It would be a comparatively easy matter to bait the sharks within

63

range of the lens. But which of the men with us would fight these cannibals of the sea?

At last, proper inducements having been offered, two of our native crew agreed to play the part of submarine gladiators. They were capable, reliable, and as nearly amphibious as human beings can be, and with them we worked out our plan of action.

A horse for bait was the positive decree of the natives. A horse we must have to obtain results. We sent men ashore to round up some decrepit beast whose days were numbered anyway. The search proved futile. We advertised, but received no answer. We began to feel a great deal of sympathy for the king who shouted, "A horse! a horse! my kingdom for a horse!" We felt the same way.

Finally, when we had just about given up hope, we located a man who owned an old horse that was lame and had been condemned to be shot. Immediately we negotiated for the carcass. The owner was to make delivery the next morning in our yard at the waterfront.

Came the dawn. Came the man, and worst of all, came the horse! The reports of his expected demise, like Mark Twain's death, had been grossly exaggerated. No animal could be shot, it appeared, without an official British Government permit. We were in a real dilemma.

Suddenly there came the flash of spiked helmets in the sun, accompanied by the military tramp of feet, and swinging into our yard came a guard of Bahamas police in charge of an officer. They came to a halt near the horse, which was thoroughly examined and found lame. With great formality the officer read aloud to the horse the permit. A soldier handed him a pneumatic gun. With neither a murmur nor a sigh our horse sat down, then lay down, its troubles definitely over.

In the business of shark fighting, tense moments were to come. I could sense this in the looks of the men and their movements as we made preparations for the encounter at a location the grey sea tigers were known to frequent.

A crew of men had been detailed to look after our bait, which was suspended from a boom and allowed to sink down into the sea for a safe distance. First came two grey monsters, wary, circling about, baleful eyes alert, grinning teeth bared. But they were suspicious. Suddenly turning, they sped away. Soon others appeared, wrinkling their blunt snouts and rolling their eyes upward as they caught the scent of blood. They also retreated. Again and again this was repeated, but each time the sharks approached they were in greater numbers and each time they were bolder, hungrier, and more anxious to hurl themselves blindly at the tempting bait floating above our photosphere. Presently, with a rush, one great monster flashed upward with open jaws.

The men on the deck were ready for just such an emergency. Quickly they raised the boom, lifting the carcass clear of the water. Chagrined, the shark slunk back, but he lurked nearby, and when the bait was lowered again, he and his companions made a concerted rush. This time the men were not quick enough. The sharks threw themselves upon the meat, tearing at it, shaking it as a terrier shakes a rat, gulping down great mouthfuls. Once they had tasted it, they forgot all caution, all suspicion. They had but one urge, and when the bait was lifted and they were baffled, they became obsessed with a maniacal fury and snapped and tore blindly at one another. Good, the madder they became, the better for us, the more savage would they appear in our picture, and the more thrilling would be the final scene of battle.

The human shark fighters appeared quite unconcerned about the ravenous beasts. While the sharks were being goaded into a frenzy, their human antagonists were rubbing oil into their black skins, the younger diving boys gazing at them in awe and admiration. Time for action had come. Summoning one of them, I told him all was ready, to choose his moment and go for it. Pointing down through the clear water, I warned him to be sure and stage his duel in front of the window or all our work would be lost. I explained that he must start when his intended victim was in position. It was not a simple matter even for a

67

person who understood the limitation of our camera movements within the photosphere, and I could see that such details meant little to this native, who, never in his life, had even seen a motion picture. It was like ordering a pugilist to be in a certain definite spot at a certain moment when he dealt the k.o. to his opponent in the ring. The diver had a much more difficult feat to perform.

The next instant there was a splash. The man was gone. The camera was started. But there was no battle under the sea. Gesticulating wildly, the diver was feinting, shadow-boxing, knife in hand. Then he shot to the surface and clambered out.

Again we lowered the bait while the diver waited, tense, gazing downward through the water like a hungry fish hawk, keen and eager for his prey. Sharks were now cruising about. The time had come. Grasping his long-bladed knife in his teeth, he dived. We watched tense, thrilled, excited. Like a skilled matador in the bull-ring, the man was placing himself in position to strike home a death blow, and, like a wary bull, the shark was doing the same.

They circled about, moving quickly first one way and then another. A moment more and both antagonists had swung far out of the range of the camera. We yelled. We shouted. It did no good. He could not hear us, and even if he could, it would not have helped matters. It was too late for him to change his tactics.

69

"The diver drove his knife up to the hilt into his enemy"
PICTURE OF A SHARK FIGHT TAKEN FROM THE PHOTOSPHERE

The position of the shark controlled matters down there. Hauling wildly at the gear, sweating, shouting, our crew fought madly to swing the vessel and bring the photosphere into position. But affairs moved swiftly. With a sudden forward dash, the diver drove his knife up to the hilt into his enemy. It was a wonderful and spectacular feat, but completely lost to the camera!

The diver bobbed up, grinning and triumphant. He danced on deck and boasted of his prowess. He had killed a shark, and he went below well satisfied with his day's work. He was through.

There was nothing to do but try it all over again with the other diver. Somehow I hadn't much confidence in this fellow. However, I repeated my warnings and instructions, and as he had watched the other man, I felt that he should understand just what was required of him. He announced that he was ready. Again the bait was lowered. For a moment we waited. Then, knife in teeth, over he went. Cautiously he moved, watchful, alert. A shark spotted him and made a rush. That was enough. Up he shot for safety, with the shark at his heels. Reaching the dead horse, which we were purposely keeping out of our picture, the diver used it as a shield, dodging about, evading the snapping teeth of the shark by inches, stark terror on his face. As a shark fighter he was an utter wash-out, but as a comedian he was a riot. But we wanted to film drama, not comedy.

Wearily I looked about for another diver, but the men had vanished. I found them concealed in the hold, and one glance at their faces was enough. There was no fight in them. It would be hopeless to ask for volunteers.

Failure! Utter failure after all our preparations and trouble. We seemed to have reached the end of our resources. A shark fight without a fighter was impossible, and we had no fighter. Utterly depressed and discouraged, I seated myself on the capstan. I had given my word that we would film a shark fight and we had failed. We had shot nearly two miles of film and all we needed were a few yards more, a few yards that might mean overwhelming success. They would be the punch we needed to put the whole thing over.

Suddenly I was inspired. I would get that picture. I would fight the shark myself!

I pulled off my clothing, cut short the legs of my thin trousers, and borrowed a long-bladed native shark knife. If a Bahaman negro could fight a shark, I could. I was as good a swimmer as any of the men, I was stronger and more physically fit than any of the natives. Moreover, I had watched every movement, every feint, every turn and twist of the diver who had killed the shark. Possibly I was over-confident. Probably, having become so accustomed to seeing the monsters swimming about separated from me by an inch or two of glass, I had lost man's instinctive terror of the sea tigers.

71

But by watching sharks in their natural habitat, under all sorts of conditions, I had acquired a deep knowledge of their ways and motions, their psychology and their limitations. At any rate, I felt no fear, no dread of meeting a man-eater face to face. Naturally I was a bit excited and thrilled at the prospect before me.

Of one thing, though, I was certain. I would make a good scene of it, no matter what happened. I would not spoil the show by getting beyond the camera's vision.

Walking aft, I called all hands on deck and told them of my decision. Eyes rolled. Mouths opened in amazement. No one had ever heard of a white man attempting the feat. I was going to my death, they felt certain. But they rubbed me down with their oil, which they declared was a secret compound. Perhaps it was, for I have never smelled anything to equal it.

Below in the watery arena I could count the sharks. Twelve great brutes! If only one more would arrive. If only they would total my lucky number—thirteen!

I dived, but only for rehearsal. The first native diver had been wise. I would follow his example—take a look about—go through the pantomime. I didn't rehearse very long. It wasn't so comfortable after all down there with those skulking grey forms on every side. Back once more on the surface, the stunt began to fascinate me. I shouted the signal for camera and waited—watching for a shark to appear in the area covered by the lens.

There he was! I flashed into action. Down through the water I plunged and swam. With a sweep of an arm, I veered to one side and the next instant was beneath the shark. What a monster he was! But I had no time to dwell on this. No time to repent of my hare-brained adventure. It was too late for retreat, for with a flirt of his tail the shark had turned and was dashing open-mouthed at me!

But even in that tense moment I caught a glimpse of the window of the chamber. I saw the men feverishly working with the camera, and I knew that, whatever happened in the next few seconds, they at least would get the picture of pictures.

My lungs seemed bursting. I had been under water longer than ever before. Now the great grey body was almost upon me. I remembered the native diver's trick. Veering aside, I grasped the monster's fin, felt my hand close upon it. With a twist, I was under the livid white belly at the spot I was trying to reach. With all my remaining strength I struck. A quivering thrill raced up my arm as I felt the blade bury itself to the hilt in the flesh, and the next moment I was swung right and left by a lashing body. Then a blur, confusion—chaos. I believed I was swimming desperately, striving madly to reach the surface, but I couldn't be sure. Everything seemed hazy, indistinct!

73

Hands slapping my back brought me back to reality with a jerk. Somehow I had managed to reach the deck. Everyone was shouting, and congratulating me. I had killed the shark!

Still panting from exertion, my head in a whirl, I slid down the tube in time to witness the end of the shark. With upturned belly gleaming in the wavering sunlight filtering through the waters, the dead monster was drifting away. Its companion sucker-fish was nibbling at the bloody flesh about the gaping wound over the heart—a cold-blooded cannibal devouring the flesh of his recent cannibal host.

A week later we boarded the steamer for New York, our precious film guarded like a chest of gold.

There was much to be done before the results of our expedition could be shown to the world. Five weeks in the cutting-room and laboratory found us with a complete celluloid ribbon, six thousand feet long. Six reels of film representing all our hopes and ambitions; a tiny package a foot square.

With this box of treasure we boarded the train for Washington, D.C., where the Smithsonian Institute was to give the initial exhibition of our film. Newspapers had announced the event and the imagination of the public had been aroused. The demand for admission had been unprecedented, overwhelming the officials of the Institute. Scientists and members would fill the huge auditorium at the scheduled four o'clock showing.

There was no room for others. Still the 'phone kept ringing, as it had rung for days, with government officials and others high in position clamouring for a chance to view the undersea pictures.

Could another showing be made at noon to accommodate the overflow? It could, and off I dashed to search for the projection operator, and before noon everything was in readiness.

The attendance that noon hour was tremendous and convincing. I could not even get in myself. The great hall was taxed to capacity. Perhaps I was dreaming all this. I had had such visions on nights when I slept on a bench in the cutting-room with a bag in readiness to scoop up the priceless undersea negative in case of fire, on nights when we feverishly developed our films in the crumbling stone building in the tropics. But this wonderful crowd must be real. I found credentials in my pockets and slowly worked around to an opening where I squeezed in on my papers, to see my own show, and to witness a most amazing scene.

Working my way around the back of the audience behind men and women standing on tip-toe, I crawled up breathless to the projection booth to watch the fragile film pass through the machine. It was holding together. Five reels had run through. We were into the last one. A snap of the celluloid would be doubly awful now. Suspense would be broken, and government officials and others might realize that their lunch

75

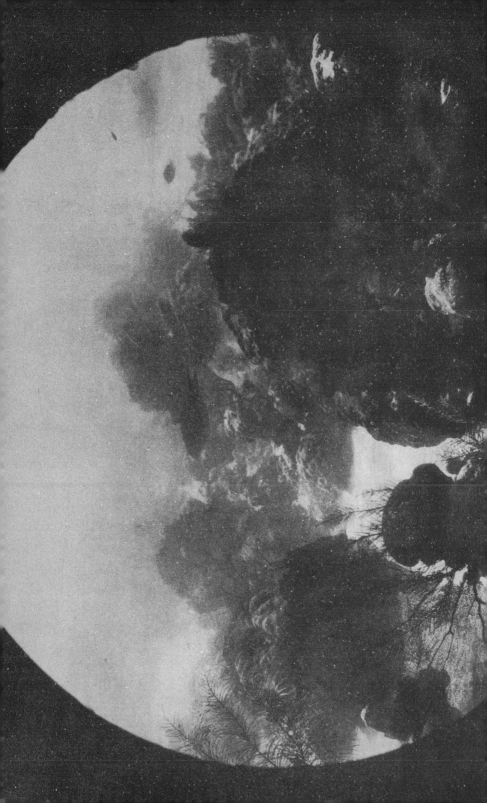

hour had long since passed. But the film spun through to the climax. Thunderous applause, music to my ears, broke the intense silence as the lights flashed on.

At the four o'clock showing a leading scientist made a brief address. He glanced over the vast audience. "At noon," he said, "I appeared here to announce that I believed we were going to see some exceptionally good pictures. Now I wish to state that I not only believe, but I know, you are about to view the most remarkable photographs that have ever been made."

It was glorious, inspiring beyond words, to hear such praise. It was ample reward for all our trials, our efforts, our labours. We had won the support and approval of the great body of scientists.

Yet another test was before us. Could we win the same approval and praise from the general public? That night we showed our film at the National Press Club which was crowded to the doors. The results were as flattering as before, and having passed the critical gathering of international correspondents with flying colours, we hurried back to New York. As a scientific accomplishment, the Washington papers hailed the showing as "films that pierced the sea, each picture an absolute revelation."

It was the verdict of the amusement seeking public however, upon which we depended for financial success. Our pictures had no story, no plot. They had to be presented as a film feature, solely on their own

77

merits, as a record of our undersea expedition. As such they must succeed or fail. A noted and experienced showman declared that the pictures would not go over. Film features were built about a love theme and sex. The people had come to expect a story, heart interest with every reel of film.

Well, there was but one way to prove whether he was right or wrong—to show the films. We would open on Broadway, bored, thrill-weary, sophisticated Broadway, the crucible of all shows. We would occupy a new theatre, with our undersea pictures as the sole attraction.

The show was a hit!

Critics exploded with superlatives of praise. "Amazing! Thrilling! Something entirely new! Something never before viewed by mankind."

We had brought the bottom of the sea to Broadway and Broadway liked it.

After taking Gotham by storm our feature ran for seven months in Chicago. London was the next citadel to fall. And so on around the world.

If there was nothing new under the sun, the "Williamson Submarine Expedition" had proved that there was something new to be seen under the sea.

Chapter IV

ALONG THE FLOOR OF THE OCEAN

COME with me under the sea. There in the great silence we can talk as wonders unfold along the ocean floor. Come just as you are, for you are not going down in a diving suit or helmet, a diving bell or any contraption that will get you wet, charge you with pressure, or cut you off from a free supply of the air above. You are going with me down the "hole in the sea" to cruise through the mysteries of the ocean —as comfortably as you would sit in your car and drive leisurely along a country road.

We arrive in a place of enchantment near the outer fringe of the West Indies. Columbus, feeling blindly for land, may have steered over these very waters. The fairyland of the aquatic world awaits us below.

The depth has been sounded and, section by section, the required length of our submarine tube has been coupled together and lowered away by our crew, and all is ready.

You can climb down with me under the sea or be lowered in a seat, but the construction of the tube forms a natural ladder. You will climb? Fine! Let's go—

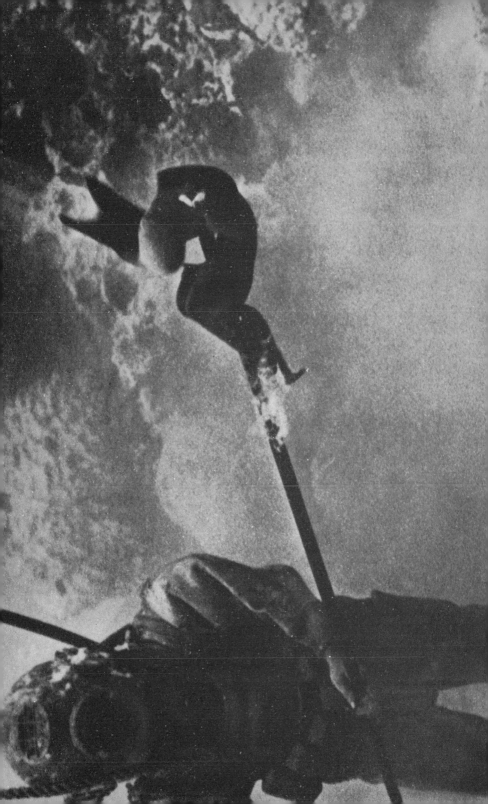

down—down we go. This is easy. We can rest awhile here, about forty feet below the surface. You can see how the water pressure affects the flexible metallic tube. It works in accordion-fashion, increasing its strength and adjusting itself to the varying pressure of the sea. The bending motion felt near the surface lessens as we descend.

It is quiet here—away from the waves at the surface.

Another forty feet down and we are in the photosphere at the bottom of the tube, thirteen fathoms deep. There is room for several more here, so we shall not be crowded. Please be seated and rest comfortably. You may smoke if you wish. There! The comforts of home! Now, to start on your journey. I draw the curtains aside so that you may see with your own eyes the mysterious floor of the ocean.

Look! What luck! We have landed right in the heart of an old wreck with only its "dead bones" remaining. I was hoping to locate it, for I passed it here once before and I know it harbours some weird fish. Our eyes are becoming accustomed to the pale light now, but I can flash on my lights if they are needed. Did you see that giant moray loop out of the rotted ribs of the wreck? His green snake-like body must have been twelve feet long. He is a species of conger eel equipped with poisonous teeth capable of shearing off a diver's arm or leg.

I can never forget the encounter between one of my

81

divers and an octopus in an old wreck like this. To see a man caught in the grasp of even one tentacle of the eight-armed monster, having possibly a reach of thirty feet, was a hair-raising thrill. It was a desperate struggle, and many slashing blows of the diver's knife were needed to sever the hold of this terrible beast of the deep.

See this huge shark glide up! It seems as if he is coming right in, driving his grey torpedo-like body toward us. If he doesn't change his course—— Good! His instinct to dodge saved our thick glass window a nasty shock, for he turned just a few inches away from it. However, you were quite safe, for I held the emergency cut-off and was prepared for any accident.

Wonderfully clear are these Bahaman waters. You can see through two or three hundred feet here, the water is so transparent. On the shallower white banks I have seen objects four hundred feet away—sometimes even farther. What a weird panorama unfolds as we drift along through the length of this rotted, shell-encrusted hulk, with lazy fish lying motionless in the shadows. Nothing seems so lifeless as the sunken wrecks of ships—once so much alive, in their days of service.

But we must watch out! The high stern looms up right in our path. That shark turned away and saved our big window, but a crash would be serious. Don't rise. We are all right. I telephone a signal—"On deck! Take up the chamber twelve feet.—All right!

82

Hold it! Lower away some. Hold steady!" Easy to handle is this "portable hole in the sea." I sit here with gauges to watch and controls to handle, while in close touch by telephone with my crew. I am the pilot, only the usual plan of piloting is inverted. On the bridge of a ship the pilot signals below. I signal up to the surface, setting the course for our vessel which carries along the "hole in the sea" and us with it, drawing up our studio or lowering it. You see, the whole invention broadly consists of three components—a surface floating vessel, a terminal work chamber, and the flexible connecting tube.

Our wreck is far behind us and I am drawing up our chamber gradually as we approach a ledge. A sea of light seems to flow over the edge of it and down the white sand incline, in effect like a waterfall. Look up! I will work a control and bend the tube round so that you may see overhead, the ceiling of the sea! There is a sight few have beheld. Millions of light beams flashing through the rippling cups of the waves at the surface, creating a rain of light, and as the shafts flash down to the sea bed, they weave a carpet of soft loops into a tangle of patterns which dance and flow on the sea floor.

Now we are over the ledge and a straight-away course is open for easy sailing. A white coral sand prairie rolling like billows—a sand that is partly coral, but sown with the impalpable dust of shells.

Do you know, there are great areas of quicksand under the sea? In developing one of my films I conceived the idea of having one of my characters, as he walked along the sea-floor, caught and drawn into the quicksand. Another diver was to arrive on the scene and effect the rescue at the last moment. The rescuer could not, of course, follow into the quicksand. He must endeavour to sweep a chain around the sinking man, and by drawing the chain and tightening it, he would come within reach of the victim.

Both divers were to be equipped with self-contained diving suits, which are diving suits that have no connection with the surface. The air supply is renewed and purified by a chemical known as oxylithe carried in the divers' containers.

We had been running short of this chemical, and the men in this scene were forced to use old charges; a dangerous practice, for when their one hour of usefulness is up, the foul gas coming from it suddenly intoxcates a diver so that, before he realizes it, he is a drunken maniac.

I set the cameras going and, sitting below here, I felt the terrible menace as the advancing diver began to sink into the gripping ooze. They had a ticklish job, yet with skilful men in the chemical suits, I had felt it was worth risking.

But I was due for a terrifying experience that might have ended in tragedy, though, strange to say, not

without a humorous side. The rescuing diver after cleverly placing the chain in the widest possible circle round the doomed man, suddenly stopped and sat down, hugging his knees like one watching a show, and apparently enjoying the exit of the man he had come to rescue. The fellow sitting there was strangely intoxicated—drunk on the ocean floor—and but for the fact that I held other divers and native swimmers in readiness for unforeseen accidents which often occurred in my peculiar work, our trapped man might have disappeared for ever. As it worked out, the "drunk" was harder to rescue than the almost victim of the quicksands.

Hello! A call from the deck. The bridge signals that a squall is coming. Don't be alarmed in the least. I've witnessed many storms from this very window under the sea. It's a great sight to look up underneath the surface when a heavy rain is on. Let us bend the tube round. We can now look up. Waves are splashing above, but on the under side they are undulating smoothly with no breaking crests. The sun is still shining and the silver rain of light comes down to us like fireworks. Suddenly the clouds shut out the sun and the heavy raindrops start to pelt the sea, penetrating for several inches, according to their size. They look like millions of lead pencils being shot into the sea and pulled back again. It is quite dark now. Flash! There goes the lightning, and close follows the muffled roll of thunder.

87

"Caught and drawn into the quicksand"
THE RESCUE OF A DIVER

Down go the waves as the rain beats them smooth. I was nearly fooled by a storm like this during my honeymoon under the sea. It started like an ordinary one, but developed into a hurricane.

I was sitting with my wife in a clustered reef with multitudes of fishes all round us. We were happy there, lost in the maze of beauty. It started to squall above, but assured by the direction of the wind, the crew gave no alarm. The signs were not those of a hurricane. But a sudden lurch of the chamber told me a heavy surge had rolled over the bottom of the sea. The fish scattered into the reef holes. Then came a long roll over the sea floor. This surge goes out like wireless, spreading its waves far in advance of a great storm. Sharks scurried by, wildly excited, while others gulped great mouthfuls of water and settled heavily to the bottom. A monster devil fish, straining with all speed, curved about with a dozen big amberjacks nesting on his broad back like circus riders.

We went to the surface to investigate and the excited voices of the coloured boys relayed the news from a smack full of native fishermen, whose eyes were popping out with fright as they flew to shelter in their frail craft. They shouted, "Big storm coming," for in some mysterious way the news had reached them from the Nassau Weather Bureau that a "tropical storm of severe intensity" was on its way. We were right in its path. Our barometer was dropping like mad.

We lost no time in getting away from the reefs to the nearest shelter with our outfit, and none too soon. Though strained almost to breaking point, we weathered the storm that took its tremendous toll in lives, and wrecked so many homes in Florida and the West Indies.

But don't let this experience worry you now. Our little squall has passed by. The sunlight again lights up the sea-floor. There's a sight coming soon that will thrill you, for I am taking you to a forest of coral. Hello! A parrot-fish pays us a visit right at our window. He is more than two feet long and must weigh twenty-five pounds. Observe the sheen of his blue-green body. His beak, like a parrot's, is as hard as flint. This spells trouble. See that! He drives at the glass and cuts a Z-shaped scratch. He is fighting himself in the looking-glass, for, over this white bottom, our window acts as a mirror. If more parrot-fish get the looking-glass signal for fight, we shall have to move quickly. A school of them beat me off once before. They wheeled about in army formation and attacked my big glass window. They got madder and madder as they hit the blank wall, nose to nose with their own reflections in the glass—to them a gang as angry as they were.

What a flash of colour their bright-hued bodies made! But two weeks of polishing, with many aching arms and backs among my crew, failed to remove the scratches and a new glass had to be cast and imported,

for these deep-sea windows of mine are several inches thick. Luckily, our visiting parrot-fish has changed his mind, though you'll notice that from where he is busy over there he keeps his eye on us as he bites into the trunk of that stony coral post. His eternal appetite has stayed his fighting spirit. He is now grubbing for food, and to find it he can crack that coral just as a parrot breaks a biscuit with his beak. Imbedded in his throat is an extra set of molars with which he grinds down his diet.

The brilliant colours of tropical fish are truly a source of wonder; but now as you visit the floor of the ocean, you can observe these gaudy creatures in their natural haunts and understand why they are so highly coloured. Here the corals, sea fans, sponges and other marine growths fairly glow with colour. Scarlet, crimson, rose-pink, lilac, orange, brilliant yellow, vivid greens, blues of every shade, blend and intermingle. Against this background, swimming between the corals and sponges, the most brilliant of tropical fish blend perfectly with their surroundings and change their colours to suit the environment of the moment.

'He is fighting himself in the looking-glass'
A PARROT FISH ATTACKING THE WINDOW OF THE PHOTOSPHERE

Chapter V

DEVIL FISH AND FISH DEVILS

THE term "devil fish" is applied rather indiscriminately to many inhabitants of the ocean, and often is confusing and misleading. The giant oceanic sunfish—a moonshaped, tailless, harmless creature—is often called devil fish, but the true devil fish is the giant ray or "manta." This immense creature resembles the common ray or skate in form, but attains enormous size, often measuring twelve or fifteen feet across its flat body and great wing-like fins. On either side of the head are short flexible arms. It is equipped with a long, whip-like tail and, with its coal-black upper surface and white belly, has such a dangerous, demoniac appearance that it has been named devil fish. But despite its devilish aspect the manta is a harmless, peaceable creature, unless harpooned or captured, when its enormous size and strength render it a dangerous antagonist. Normally these giant rays live in fairly shallow water, feeding and resting on the bottom or swimming about with a peculiar flapping motion like gigantic undersea bats. Often, however, they amuse themselves by leaping from the sea, springing high in the air, flapping their "wings" and falling with tremendous splashes. When captured they often resort to this high-jumping ability, and, throwing themselves up from the sea, crash down on the boat and the luckless fishermen. It would be far better if these weird fishes were called fish devils rather than devil fish, for to most persons the term devil fish brings visions of the octopus or the giant squid. Both are cuttle-fish, cephalopods, and are first cousins to the pearly nautilus and the argonaut famed in poetry. But they differ widely in appearance and habits. The squids have long, cigar-shaped bodies, tapering to a point and equipped with lateral fins like the horizontal rudders of a submarine. They possess ten arms, eight of which are short and stout and completely covered with suckers on the inner surface, while the other two are very long and oar-shaped with suckers only on the broad tips. Like the octopus, they propel themselves backward by ejecting a stream of water from a tube or siphon between the head and body, and, like the octopus, they can eject a great quantity of ink or sepia with which to cloud the water and enable them to escape from their enemies. Small squids are common in all seas, but the giant squids, which by the way, form the chief diet of sperm whales, are inhabitants of the ocean's great depths. No one can say to what enormous size these giant creatures may grow, but specimens washed ashore at Newfoundland, and figured and described by the late Professor

A. E. Verrill, the eminent zoologist of Yale University, measured nearly sixty feet from the tip of the tentacles to the tail, and weighed several tons each. Dr. Paul Bartsch, curator of marine life at the Smithsonian Institute, states that the single tentacle of one squid found measured sixty feet in length. The spread of this creature's outflung tentacles may have been one hundred and twenty feet. In the opinion of Dr. Bartsch, such great squids skimming just below the surface of the sea and making their two longest feelers weave across the sea surface, have given rise to the reports of sighting giant sea-serpents. Such monsters are true devils of the sea and would be terrible menaces to divers and all who dared invade their undersea world. Fortunately for mankind, however, they seldom rise to the surface and are incapable of surviving long except at depths of half a mile or more below the surface. The octopus, on the other hand, dwells in shallow water everywhere in tropical and semi-tropical seas. There are many species, ranging in size from a few inches across to gigantic monsters; but all are alike in general form and habits. Their bodies are round or pear-shaped. They have no fins and they possess eight tentacles, all of about equal length and all with suckers on the under side throughout their entire length.

Both the squid and the octopus employ their tentacles for crawling about and for capturing and holding their prey, which is then bitten into fragments by the creatures' powerful parrot-like beaks. The food of the octopus consists mainly of crabs, crayfish and such fish as it can capture, but it does not hesitate to attack any living thing that comes within range of its cold, saucer-like eyes. This is not because it is courageous, but because it possesses practically no brains. Neither does its body enclose a skeleton. It is all gristle and pulp, yet it has tremendous strength and endurance, and is most tenacious of life. Even a small octopus can put up a terrific fight as long as it is in the water; but once removed from their native element, the creatures soon become exhausted. One scientist of my acquaintance, who was collecting marine life in the Bermudas, had assured his assistants that if an octopus were grasped firmly by the neck it would be helpless and would soon tire out. A short time afterward the professor was collecting in knee-deep water when he caught sight of a four-foot octopus retreating into its hole. Leaping forward he succeeded in seizing the creature and, to demonstrate his theory, he raised the octopus on high, firmly grasped at the neck, with the writhing tentacles entwining his arm. Suddenly it ejected a stream of ink full in the scientist's face. Startled, his eyes blinded and smarting, the professor sprang backwards, stumbled, and the next moment was floundering in the shallow water, struggling madly with the octopus whose activity and strength had been trebled the instant it had touched water, and whose outflung tentacles had

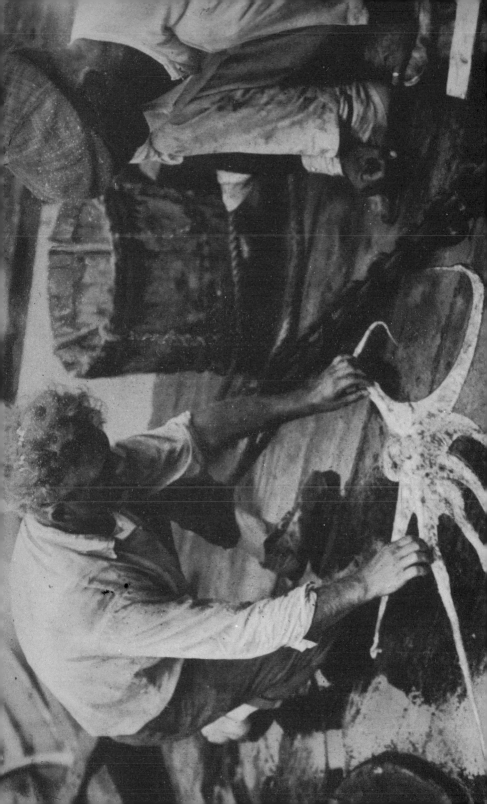

encircled its captor's neck. The scientist, however, was not one to be worsted by a four-foot cephalopod, and he had the courage of his convictions. Not for a moment did he release his grip on the creature's neck, and at last, regaining his feet, he held the beast at arm's length until the tentacles relaxed, the pulpy body sagged, and the triumphant scientist dropped his inert **captive** into a collecting receptacle. If a four-foot octopus—a mere baby—is capable of such a fight, imagine, if you can, what a terrible enemy a ten or twenty-foot specimen would prove! In most countries where the octopus is plentiful, the creatures are considered excellent food, and are always found on sale in the fish markets. But native fishermen make no attempts to capture their prey alive. They deem it safer and surer to spear them, or otherwise put them to death.

From earliest times the octopus has been the theme of innumerable thrilling and breath-taking tales of the sea. The ancients narrated weirdly terrible stories of the "Kraken," a monster of the deep as large as a small island, which attacked ships, and with its gigantic arms seized upon the masts and drew the vessels down beneath the waves where it devoured the members of the crew. There is no doubt that the mythical, legendary Kraken was the giant octopus of fact. Victor Hugo in *Toilers of the Sea* featured the loathsome, horrible creature. Jules Verne vividly described a ghastly battle with a huge octopus. In the West Indies,

97

If a four-foot octopus is capable of such a fight . . ."

the natives speak in lowered tones of certain bays and channels where no man dares to venture after nightfall because of giant octopuses that steal forth from their undersea lairs, and, crawling up the sides of the vessels, seize the terrified crew and drag them down to the depths.

Who dares to say what in these tales is fiction and what is fact? Who can safely assert that the Kraken was purely a legendary creature? What person, even if a matter-of-fact scientist, can positively declare that immense octopuses do not attack and destroy human beings? Personally, I believe that many such tales are true, that they are only slightly exaggerated, if at all. For I have seen these monsters of the deep in their undersea haunts and know from experience what terrible, almost irresistible creatures they are. It is impossible even to conjecture what size an octopus may attain. Specimens measuring thirty feet from tip to tip of tentacles have been captured in the Gulf of California. Exact life-sized reproductions of these awful monsters may be seen in museums all over the world. Against such a devil of the deep, a man would stand no chance in a hand-to-hand struggle, yet these are by no means the largest individuals of their race. About thirty years ago the battered and mutilated remains of a stupendous octopus were found washed ashore by a storm upon a Florida beach. This immense mass of gristle and muscle weighed nearly half a ton, and, judging from the relative proportions of ordinary specimens, this gigantic devil fish must have possessed tentacles fully sixty feet in length. Picture, if you can, such an indescribably horrible monster. Try to visualize that thousand-pound slimy body—pulsing in livid green, sickly grey, dull red and mottled corpse-like white— with huge staring green eyes above the sixty-foot tentacles armed with thousands of sucker disks as large as saucers! Strive to imagine coming upon the horrid monster in the depths of the sea, meeting him face-to-face lurking behind some coral reef or hidden within the black depths of the hold of a sunken ship. Think of the terror, the awful paralysing fear of a diver coming upon it while seeking to salvage treasure from some foundered wreck. Awkward and hampered by his diving suit, forced to move slowly, deliberately, beneath the water, the diver would stand no chance. Before he could signal frantically to be drawn up to the surface, if in an ordinary suit, or could release his compressed air and so rise to the surface, if wearing a self-contained suit, one of those huge tentacles would dart forth and, like a giant anaconda, wind itself about the unfortunate man. Held in the grip of hundreds of great suckers, encircled by the coiling tentacles, the diver would be as helpless as a rabbit in the grip of a boa constrictor. Even if he drew a knife or hatchet and chopped savagely with all his strength at the snake-like tentacle, his blows would be impotent, for instantly another and another gigantic sucker-clad arm would be flung about him. With arms and legs pinioned, unable even to struggle, the hapless man would be dragged toward those baleful cold orbs, toward the huge black beak, opening and closing, its razor-sharp edges whetted and ready to shear through garments, flesh and bone, to bite deep into his vitals, to devour him alive! No power could save him. The most desperate efforts of his fellows to drag him to the surface would be of no avail. The thousand-pound body, anchored securely by its tentacles, would be as immovable as the bottom of the ocean itself. The awed and terrified men above would never know, might never even suspect, his fate. The parted life-line and air tube would be mute evidence of some tragedy beneath the sea. A dull red stain rising to the surface, and bubbles frothy with blood would tell the anxious, white-faced watchers that their comrade had met with some tragic end. But the chances are they would think he had been killed by sharks, never suspecting, never dreaming that a living terror lurked amid the shadowy deep under the keel of their boat.

Many a diver has vanished for ever under the sea. Many a vessel has disappeared with never a trace when no raging storm lashed the sea to fury, when no reef or rock was near. Who can say that these mysteries of the sea, these unexplained tragedies, were not brought about by gigantic devil fish, veritable Krakens? Because

no one has actually seen such a monster of the deep does
not prove that they do not exist. Only by a real miracle
could a human being see such a creature and live to tell
the tale. And we know from positive and indisputable
evidence that such gigantic and fearsome beings do
exist somewhere in the ocean's depths. But no sixty-
foot octopus is needed to prove a deadly, a terrible
menace to humans who invade the realm beneath the
sea, and strive to wrest the secrets of the ocean from
Father Neptune. A thirty-foot devil fish, even an
octopus with ten-foot tentacles would prove capable of
overpowering and destroying the strongest, bravest
man. And such creatures do exist, not in the unfathom-
able depths of the ocean, not as rare, isolated individuals,
but by scores in comparatively shallow water. I have
seen many of these horrible creatures during my
twenty years under the sea. Filled with a strange
fascination, combined with indescribable loathing, I
have watched these devils of the sea in their native
haunts. I have seen them seize, kill and devour their
prey, and although safely ensconced behind the thick
glass of my window, I have never been able to overcome a feeling of dread, of instinctive fear, at the sight
of these eight-armed demons. A man-eating shark, a
giant poison-fanged moray, a murderous barracuda,
appear harmless, innocent, friendly and even attractive,
when compared to the octopus. No words can adequately describe the sickening terror one feels when

from some dark mysterious lair, the great lidless eyes of the octopus stare at one. People speak of the cold eyes of fishes, of the cruel, baleful eyes of sharks, but in all creation there are no eyes like those of the octopus. They are everything that is horrible. Dead eyes. The eyes of a corpse through which the demon peers forth, unearthly, expressionless, yet filled with such bestial malignancy that one's very soul seems to shrink beneath their gaze, and cold perspiration beads the brow. And in their cold green depths lies hypnotic power. As a long, writhing tentacle stretches forth, its tip waving about feeling for a grip, the hapless victim seems paralysed, powerless to move. Not until the awful arms have twined themselves about his body and the great suckers have fastened themselves immovably in place, is the spell broken.

And then it is too late to struggle or resist!

Chapter VI

THE one and only time I ever felt big and important was the first time I slipped into the ocean dressed in a diving suit. It may have been the hot half-hour preceding my immersion as I sat on the deck of the diving boat under a tropical sun while they bolted and screwed me into the ponderous lead-weighted costume, heavier by pounds than I myself; but whatever it was, I could have sworn that someone, and a big fellow at that, was sitting on my neck as I staggered over the ladder and into the sea. However, once past the zero line that separates air from water, I blew up to bigness. I was as light as a feather. My glide to the sea floor was a streamline experience; and though each of my shoes was soled with sixteen pounds of lead, I found I could stride like a giant in seven-league boots.

Every foot you descend adds a half-pound more to the pressure on every square inch of you, so at thirty feet down you are bearing the squeeze of another whole atmosphere; and that is how it goes doubling, trebling, and so on until you reach bottom, wherever that is. Your body accepts the change quite readily. The

pressure slips into your blood and tissues, it is air pressure which the pumps are forcing all through you. You are just like a motor car tire, and you are pumped up to, and over, the pressure around you. But there is one part of the anatomy—of mine in particular—that resents with a vengeance the injection of air pressure: the ear drums. Yet, apart from the stinging pressure and the subsequent "singing of crickets" in the ears for weeks, it is thrilling to get down to the sea-bed and lean to the current; to be a fully armoured diver in regulation costume, even as an amateur.

My initiation into diving came suddenly while producing one of my deep-sea dramas, "The Submarine Eye." The plot centred about the contents of a safe which had gone overboard when being conveyed to a ship during a storm at sea. In the story the diver descends to the ocean's floor, locates the safe which has fallen over on its back in the débris, pries open the heavy door and, bending over, prepares to extract the strong-box. Just as he is about to raise it, the massive door drops, pinning his hands, holding him as in a vise, where he struggles and writhes hour after hour, gradually weakening, gradually facing a terrible death beneath the sea, until, at the last moment, he is rescued by a native diver. When I was ready for the scene the diver who was to salvage the contents of the safe, was suddenly incapacitated, and I had no one else available to act the part convincingly. I had written the story myself and wanted "perfect" results. There was but one solution: to act the scene myself. So, leaving my camera man in the undersea studio after working out a system of signals with him, I donned a diving suit and was lowered to the bottom of the sea beside the safe. Needless to say, the safe had been prepared for the scene. Apertures large enough to admit a man's hands had been cut in the edge of the door jamb, and these had been covered with flat rubber bands, so that they were invisible and would not show in the picture. But I found they were so well concealed that I could not even see them myself, and so I was obliged to resort to the sense of touch for finding where to place my hands when the door slammed shut. As I could not interrupt the action by stopping to feel about once the camera was started, I rehearsed the whole scene carefully and was ready to go ahead with the filming of it the following day. Once more I dropped through the water, clad in my diving regalia. Once again I approached the shell-encrusted safe. Slowly I walked about it, examining it, knocking the accumulation of marine growths from its surface and door while the camera clicked away behind the window of the photosphere. Inserting my crowbar in the edge of the door, I prised. The lid slowly opened. Dropping the bar, I raised the massive door high, and, leaning forward, reached within the safe for the precious strong-box. Now came the great moment. I was as tense with excitement as though I were really living the scene. Straightening up, I moved to position, ready to give the open door the jar necessary to make it close. And then—the film recorded just what happened—a shark flashed into the scene and out again, so close that the force of its passage through the water may have caused the heavy iron door to fall unexpectedly; at all events, before I had time to place my hands in the rubber-lined apertures, it shut! Faint with the shock of it, I found my hands held fast under its edge. I was pinioned, incapable of signalling to the crew above, unable even to let the camera man know of my predicament, for my signals were to be given with my hands. The shark had brought realism to the scene with a vengeance. I was trapped exactly as the diver of the story had been trapped! Sweat trickled down my forehead into my eyes. Then I realized that the camera was recording everything. I must give it action. My hands did not seem to be seriously injured; at least I hoped not. I had no need to worry about being rescued. In the story the trapped diver struggled for hours, but such lapse of time had no place in the actual filming. The native diver who was to come to my rescue had instructions to appear in less than ten minutes. With this cheering thought I instantly began to struggle and strain. I had no need to act the part. I could feel every bit of it. And never have I known greater relief, greater joy, than when the black diver came swimming down, picked up the bar, pried open the safe door and released my numbed hands and wrists. Needless to say, the pictures of that scene were realism itself.

It is a topsy-turvy world, this realm of the diver. What means something of vital importance to the man up above may mean nothing at all to the man in the suit down below. A humorous experience of mine will explain this.

The sky was overcast and we were busy on some of our painstaking preparations before "shooting" a scene. I had gone down in a diving suit to do some special work on an old wreck. For picture purposes I wanted it to look even more ancient and battered. I wanted it matted with sea growth and in every detail to give the impression of having remained there for many years.

To obtain this result I chose to do a great deal of the work myself. I was getting along gloriously. I had no idea how long I had been down. There is a certain feeling of exhilaration that blots out all thought of the passage of time. You simply have no sense of time.

So it was with mingled surprise and irritation that I felt three sharp jerks on the life-line. This is the sign to come up at once. No argument. To respect this signal was imperative. Though my work was almost completed, and I was anxious to finish it, I answered the signal and immediately they started to pull me up. Soon I reached the diving ladder, and climbed out of

the sea. As my helmeted head rose above the surface, I heard a sharp patter, a tattoo on my helmet that sounded to me like riveting.

"What's the matter?" I asked as soon as my helmet was opened.

"It's raining!"

"Raining! What do I care about that," I yelled. "Screw up my face-plate, I'm going down again."

Then I realized, as I looked round at my half-drowned assistants that while I stood there perfectly dry inside my diving suit, a tropical rain-squall was pelting them unmercifully.

Another time, the unforeseen gave me some nerve-torturing moments that have never been equalled during my twenty years of adventures beneath the sea.

I was directing the undersea scenes of another of my own film productions, "Girl of the Sea." Its story was my own. I had an excellent diver who doubled for the hero, and, seated in the chamber of my photosphere with my camera man cranking beside me, I looked out at this diver at work among the ruins of a gruesome and rotting old vessel on the floor of the sea. He was making his way laboriously along the slanting deck of the wreck. Reaching a cabin door, he forced it open and reeled back into a shower of bubbles from his helmet. There, on the slimy floor, revealed by a flood of light from above, was a human skeleton. Projecting from between the ribs where they joined the spine was the handle of a murderous knife. Upon one bony finger was a curious antique ring. The entire plot of the story hinged upon the diver's recovery of the ring and the knife. But it seemed difficult for this man, locked in a diving suit—a grotesque and unwieldy outfit—to put into convincing action the intimate details of the scene. His action up to the point of the close-ups had been splendid, but here he was fumbling the knife and the ring out of line with the camera. Again and again the action was repeated, and each time it was worse than before. At last, realizing that it was hopeless to expect satisfactory results in this way, I decided to do the close-ups myself. Hurrying to the surface, for we had wasted much valuable time already, I seized upon the first suit at hand, an old one, long unused, which had recently come from the storehouse ashore. Dropping into the sea, I changed places with the diver. I was alone in the pale-green depths. No sound, other than the throb of the air-valves, broke the death-like silence. Despite the fact that I knew every detail of the eerie spot, despite the fact that I had planned it all, I felt awed, tense with nerves on edge, exactly as I had imagined the man whose part I was acting, should feel. Sinking to my knees, I reached for the handle of the knife. As I did so, a spotted moray wormed its sinuous way between the legs of the skeleton, arousing all my loathing for those snaky creatures, and I recoiled in horror. Nor was I acting. I was the man of the part, though dread and hatred of creeping things rather than the grinning skull and disintegrating human bones actuated my sensations and movements. Cautiously I withdrew the knife, and, moving closer, I lifted the skeleton hand to remove the ring from the dead man's finger. At this tense, exciting moment something indescribably hideous happened!

Inside my copper helmet I felt something moving! Something was crawling—creeping through my hair. I was paralysed with the horror of it. I wanted to tear the helmet from my head; yet, in the midst of my terror at the thing now moving with pin-pointed feet down my forehead, was the driving thought that I must not —could not—spoil the film; that no matter what, I must go on. Now the fearsome thing was crawling over my left eye, down my nose, I could see it! My hair seemed to stand on end. I felt cold all over. The thing was a scorpion! In mental torture I controlled a desire to dash my head against the inside of the helmet and try to crush the venomous creature. But I knew that at the slightest movement it might bury its poisonous sting in my flesh—even in my eye. Though I might crush it, it still could blind or wound me in its death throes. No, I must be cool, must control myself. With unspeakable relief I felt the creature crawl back into my hair. Irritating, maddening, loathsome as it was, it had not harmed me. If undisturbed, it might remain peaceably inclined until I reached the surface and the helmet could be removed. And all this time, while my mind was numb with dread of the scorpion imprisoned in my helmet, I was going through with my part, acting out the scene, while the cameras clicked away and the operators marvelled at the vivid realism of my acting, little dreaming that it was a scorpion in my helmet that was filling me with the emotions I was exhibiting.

Only twenty minutes had elapsed between the time when I was lowered to the old wreck and when I was drawn to the surface, but to me the time seemed years, ages, an eternity.

When at last the helmet was lifted and I told my story, I was greeted with questioning looks from my men. There was no sign of a scorpion anywhere! Nothing, however, would convince me that this awful creature had been a figment of an overwrought mind. It had been far too vivid, too real, even for a nightmare. I examined the interior of the helmet. Nothing there. Then I had a sudden inspiration. From the air-tube at the back of the helmet several flat channels lead in various directions, their purpose being ·to distribute the air throughout the helmet instead of rushing it in at one place. And when a blast of air was forced through these channels, out came the scorpion.

To this day I do not know how I escaped being stung. One naturalist to whom I related the story expressed the opinion that in all probability the scorpion was affected by the air pressure, and, drugged and half torpid from the unusual conditions, was practically harmless at the time. But whatever the explanation, it taught me a lesson—never to put on a diving suit that had been stored away, without proper examination first.

If confusion can result in the system of signalling to divers with lifelines and air-pipes while they are submerged, the difficulty multiplies when the divers you wish to direct are off on a stroll over the wide sea-floor in self-contained suits with no kind of connection; free men of the under-sea, out on their own.

In the filming of Jules Verne's wonder story, *Twenty Thousand Leagues Under the Sea*, I was beset with such difficulties. I could communicate with my divers only by means of a few possible signals—a deaf-and-dumb language. But at the very end came an astounding discovery.

Already most of the company had left for their homes in the United States and the divers who had "made" the photoplay under the sea were impatient, chafing also to be off. I had told them I reckoned on their getting through in time to sail on that day's boat. They assembled below the sea for their final act. As they stood there awaiting the signal to begin I thought longingly, as I had a hundred times before, of the advantages of working in a land studio where one could talk to the actors and shout instructions to meet changing conditions. They kept changing this day.

Again and again the signal was given to start. Again and again something went wrong, and all had to be done over again.

The divers were growing increasingly impatient, more and more disgusted with having to serve as movie actors; more and more anxious to finish their work, swap diving suits for ordinary clothes, board the steamer, and head for New York. But the scene must be taken or the thousands of feet of precious film—all our months of work, and a fortune in expenditure—would be as good as thrown away. And then, faintly, through the water came the unmistakable sound of the steamer's farewell whistle. For an instant the divers stood tense. They had missed the boat! Then suddenly, unexpectedly, amazingly, a human voice broke through the silence of the ocean's depths.

"Hey, Crilley, there goes your boat!"

Clear and distinct as if in the open air came the words in Jack Gardner's voice. I gazed at the diver unbelievingly. Was it possible? Was—but before I could frame the question, "The hell you say," exclaimed Crilley. "And my wife's on board." The next minute the water was filled with excited voices, with expletives as the divers, suddenly and miraculously having discovered they could converse, gathered in a group and shouted and talked to one another. They were like deaf mutes with voice and hearing suddenly restored!

Gardner had solved the problem. He had made an

epochal discovery. And like so many epochal discoveries it had been made accidentally. Impatient at delay, chafing under the restraint, he had sought to ease his mind by ragging Crilley. He had removed the breathing tube of his self-contained suit from his lips and had spoken, taking a chance on breathing the foul air in his helmet. It was simple, so easy, that no one had thought of it before. No, not even marvellously clever, imaginative, far-seeing Jules Verne himself had found a way to permit his characters to converse when encased in chemical diving suits under the sea. Now that the discovery had been made, other discoveries followed rapidly. Not only could the divers converse beneath the sea; even when seated in my under-sea chamber I could hear them talking. Their voices came plainly to my ears through the thick steel walls of the photosphere. Obviously, water was a better conductor of sound than air. In all my underseas experience, I had never felt more thrilled, more elated, than on that memorable day when Gardner's voice broke the vast silence of the green-lit depths. However, I could not help bitterly regretting that the discovery had not been made months earlier. What difficulties might have been avoided!

The voice from the deep recalled to me the thoughts of Jules Verne's own characters as they strolled through the great under-seas, bursting to express in words their pent-up enthusiasm at the wonders and marvels unfolding before them.

"Why could I not communicate?" exclaimed Professor Arronax. "For aught I knew Captain Nemo and his companions might be able to exchange thoughts by means of signs previously agreed upon. So for want of better, I talked to myself. There was nothing wanting but the charm of conversation; but impossible to speak, impossible to answer, I could only put my great copper head close to my companions."

Strangely enough it was Gardner who had impersonated Professor Arronax in that very scene.

Perhaps it was Jules Verne himself, sending suggestions from the beyond, striving to help us, who had brought his great work to realization in our film.

Chapter VII

PRODUCTION NUMBER TWO

AS surely as undersea movies followed my first
still photographs, we were destined to film Jules
Verne's world-famous story, *Twenty Thousand Leagues
Under the Sea.* This golden opportunity presented itself immediately after I had startled the world with the
magic of motion pictures from the bottom of the sea.

You will have to get back to Broadway—the Broadway of 1915—to feel the public enthusiasm that was
carrying us along to success in the rising industry of
moving pictures.

Growing with us was something of even greater
moment—the distant rumblings of the World War.
The United States was two years away from it, yet
close enough for the public to begin to sense the
terrible menace of one of the outstanding features of
the war, the deadly submarine. Death was stalking
beneath the sea; striking from the dark. Stark tragedy
was being enacted thousands of miles away, yet close
enough to fire the imagination of the most blasé
Broadwayite.

But in spite of such shocking revelations, Broadway

was Broadway. It takes more than a war to quench the spirit of the show world. Entertainment is carried to the front-line trenches. In periods of unrest and uncertainty, diversion, bringing laughter and tears, affords a relief, a safety valve. Regardless of the horror and tragedy it was producing daily, there were elements of romance in this submarine warfare. There was the sport of the hunter and the hunted. To expose it would be a hit!

And there we were with the answer, Jules Verne's master story right in our hands. We were in on the news. Doubly blessed, we were right on Broadway, with "The Williamson Submarine Expedition" which, while it gave only a peep into the wonders and mysteries of the deep, was a revelation and sensational entertainment. With the Jules Verne story dominated by the fascinating Captain Nemo we could go on into the depths—to the bottom of the ocean.

It was great to be in on such a boom, to be able to give the public what it wanted, a real photoplay, a human drama, different from our current picture which had no plot, no story—just the drift of a unique expedition. Now we could play human emotions against the throbbing background of the mysterious undersea world.

To vindicate Verne, the dreamer, was my problem as I set out to supervise the production of the picture—to make Jules Verne's dream come true. But where were the unique and extraordinary props?

For our venture we needed a submarine to represent the *Nautilus*, a ship for the *Abraham Lincoln*, a yacht to be torpedoed, submarine guns to be used in hunting game in the coral jungles under the sea, and of vital importance, diving suits which would enable men to wander over the sea-floor without life-lines, air-tubes or other connection with the surface.

It is odd how we find what we seek. I had scarcely started my search when I learned from a chance-met veteran diver that suits such as I needed were being manufactured in England, and, better still, that a representative of the manufacturer was at that very time at the Brooklyn Navy Yard, instructing naval divers in the use of these suits. I lost no time in getting in touch with the agent, and inviting him with Chief Gunner Stillson, who was conducting the diving school, to dine with me, I explained the situation. The result was that within two days all details had been arranged, fifteen suits had been ordered and, with the co-operation of the Navy Department, I had engaged a number of the best divers in the United States to sail with me for the Bahama Islands within a month.

In the meantime I was racking my brain and conferring with arms experts regarding undersea guns. But here I drew a blank. I decided then to tackle the problem of the submarine boat. That, I felt, would be easy. There was no mystery, no lack of information, on that subject. No doubt there were plenty of obsolete submarines knocking about that would serve as the *Nautilus*. But my confidence was soon punctured. I found it impossible to get hold of a submarine. There was not on the market one in which the most foolhardy would risk his life. With war raging and German U-boats combing the seas the Navy would no more think of lending a submarine, no matter how out of date, than of lending a first-class battleship. So much for being "in the news." Having failed to get the submarine, I determined to try my luck on something really easy; procuring an old tub to do duty as the frigate *Abraham Lincoln*, and an out-of-date yacht to be sacrificed to the vengeance of Captain Nemo.

Ships and yachts there were a-plenty. The wartime demand for anything that would float had not yet arisen. None, however, would serve my purpose, for all lacked one most important feature. Many were old, but not old enough. Jules Verne's story had been written fifty years earlier and in fifty years maritime modes, ships' hulls, rigging and details had undergone much change. Yet the frigate and the yacht of my picture must both bear the earmarks of an era fifty years gone by. At last, after an almost endless search, I found an old brig which, with alterations, might serve as the *Abraham Lincoln*. By sheer good luck, also, I came upon a long-unused yacht that might have been a sister ship of the vessel we needed. Fortune seemed to smile again. I was as tickled as a cat with two tails.

With the divers, the frigate and the yacht in readiness, we were all ready to sail for the Bahamas. Among the divers was a young fellow of average height, and with no evidence of great strength and stamina, Frank Crilley. Crilley was later to be acknowledged as a master of his profession, with a record of 315 feet below the surface. He was to make this record within the month, nearly 6,000 miles from where I expected him to be working for me.

Here again Fate stepped in and wrecked my plans for the time being. The United States submarine "F-4" went to the bottom at Hawaii. All but two of my divers were members of the United States Navy, and were immediately ordered to the scene of the tragedy. There I was, with fifteen costly self-contained diving-suits on my hands and only two divers with which to fill them. These two were Jack Gardner and Chin Chin, who had had some experience with self-contained diving-suits in the British Navy. Through them I learned of another experienced chemical diver, Tuck, who was in the Gulf of Mexico salvaging a wreck. To be sure, I needed fifteen men, but three were better than none, and I felt sure that among the expert swimmers and divers of the West Indies I could recruit volunteers who could be instructed in the use of these special suits. I was still minus a submarine and undersea guns, but had come to the conclusion that the only way to obtain a submarine was to build one, and that I should somehow solve the problem of the guns. I should also need a balloon to be used in that part of the story we were borrowing from *The Mysterious Island*—sequel to *Twenty Thousand Leagues Under the Sea*—to build up the story. But that didn't trouble me—not at this time. My province was beneath the sea, not above it. It would be a simple matter, I thought, to hire a balloonist and to film the ascension when the need arose.

There was nothing to keep me longer in New York, so with my crew and equipment I set sail for the Bahamas, having cabled the diver, Tuck, to meet me there.

Reaching the Bahamas, I found no difficulty in finding volunteers to act the part of Nemo's crew and, with my three professional divers, I started a school to instruct them in the use of the self-contained suits. These diving-suits were of two types: complete suits covering the entire body, and "escape" suits which enclose only the head and upper portion of the body. In the escape suit there is nothing to keep the water out other than the air contained in the helmet, which becomes so compressed that it holds the water back at the region of the diver's chin. When bending forward or sideways, the breathing-tube must be kept between the diver's teeth to prevent the water from wetting the dangerous charge.

On the morning of our first demonstration and lesson for the benefit of the dozen promising young native pupils who were grouped about, pop-eyed with

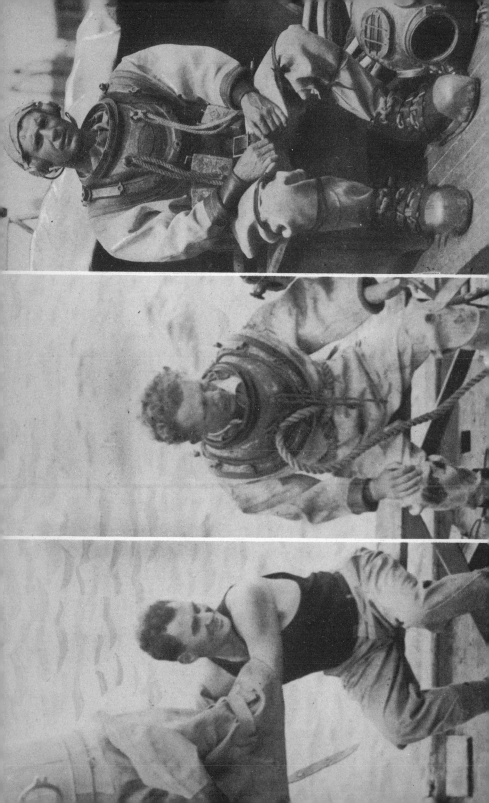

interest, Gardner put on a full suit and Tuck donned an escape suit. In the scenes which were to be filmed, it would be necessary for Tuck to struggle and tumble about, and I wanted him to get familiar with the new type of suit and to become accustomed to having water sloshing about his mouthpiece inside his helmet. I explained everything to him, warning him to be careful and pointing out the danger of letting the breathing-tube slip from his mouth.

The twelve local pupils listened and watched intently. They were all expert swimmers and at home in the water, but the sight of these odd diving-suits with their glistening metal fittings filled them with excitement. They were eager for a chance to put on the suits and walk the bottom of the sea with the professionals. As Tuck started to descend, I suggested that he use a life-line. This he declined to do. It was evident he considered himself too much of a professional diver to take precautions like an amateur. A moment later he disappeared under the sea. I did not expect him back within a half-hour as his chemical charge was good for an hour, unless he struggled too vigorously and by breathing heavily should shorten the life of the chemical. I had complete confidence in him, and busied myself with Gardner and the others.

Some fifteen minutes later a shout from an onlooker interrupted our work and, gazing seaward, we saw Tuck on the surface, floundering about. Was something

THREE DIVERS—
JACK GARDNER, THE AUTHOR AND FRANK CRILLEY

wrong? There was no scene that called for a diver struggling on top of the sea. With my company doctor, his instruments and a pulmotor which I had fortunately provided, I leaped into a boat and pulled frantically for the struggling man. As we dragged him from the sea and opened his face-plate, a cloud of blue smoke poured from his helmet. Stripping off his suit we were horrified to find him unconscious, his face a ghastly black. For a moment we thought him dead, but found that his heart still beat. After twenty minutes of strenuous effort to revive him, he started to regain consciousness, raving in delirium about seeing "beautiful ladies" and that everything was "beautiful and blue." I knew then that he was coming out of it. It had been a close call and only Tuck's presence of mind had saved him. Before putting on the suit he had neglected to clean the breathing-tube round the mouthpiece, and in turning about in the water, a tiny granule of oxylithe which had lodged on the tube under his lip had become wet and had burned into his flesh like molten lead. The excruciating pain had caused him to spit the tube out of his mouth. Instantly the water rushed into the oxylithe and the deadly gas from the chemical filled the helmet. Choking and rapidly losing consciousness he yet kept his head, forcing his brain and hands to action, realizing that his one hope was to reach the surface of the sea and the air. Fumbling blindly, he had striven to open the taps of his emergency tanks of compressed air, one of which would fill his lifebelt, while the other would inflate his suit and cause him to rise. He could not open the valves, however, because by now he was on the verge of unconsciousness. Only the primal instinct for self-preservation burned in his reeling brain. Automatically his fingers tore at the weighted belt around his waist, and released it. With a desperate effort he managed to take off one of his lead-soled shoes. This saved his life, for the release of its weight, together with that of the lead-weighted belt, made him just buoyant enough to float away from the bottom. The last he remembered was trying to remove the other shoe, and this is what he must have been doing when we first saw him at the surface.

Tuck was saved, but we lost all of our diving pupils. When the excitement of the rescue was over, the local talent were nowhere to be seen. They had vanished, never to return.

Fortunately, as it turned out, I did not need them. By the time I was ready for the big scenes, I had obtained the services of expert Navy divers, among them Chief Gunner Stillson.

Once the problem of divers and self-contained suits was solved, I took up that of the undersea guns. After many experiments we discovered that ordinary firearms could be used beneath the sea. We selected Springfield army rifles, using wax plugs in place of bullets. When fired under water, black gas belched from the muzzle

127

of the gun, giving the exact effect of smoke, while air bubbles appeared to mark the path of the bullet.

There was still the biggest problem of all—that of the submarine. There was only one way to get the craft, and that was to build it. Here my training in marine engineering would serve me well.

But as I started on this task, Fate dealt another blow. The yacht purchased in New York had not arrived. At last came word that the crew employed to bring it to the Bahamas had beached the vessel on an unfrequented section of the Carolina coast and had stripped it of everything of value. Quantities of equipment, props and vital supplies had been pirated; the yacht itself was a total loss. I prevailed upon my brother to take some of our trusted seamen and search the Florida coast for another yacht. None suitable was to be found between Jacksonville and Key West. At last we were forced to purchase a vessel that might be rebuilt to conform to our needs. She, too, nearly came to grief on her way down, but eventually she reached Nassau in safety; and we proceeded to rebuild the staunch craft. Bow and stern were extended. The sheer line was altered, new masts and a funnel were added, and when completed we had a yacht which would have fooled any nautical expert. Yet I sighed when I saw the bill for the alterations. To replace and to age the lost yacht had cost $25,000.

Meanwhile, the submarine was rapidly taking form

and substance. When completed she was well over 100 feet in length, and she can best be described by quoting from Jules Verne's account of the *Nautilus*.

"It was an elongated cylinder with conical ends, very like a cigar in shape . . . with iron plates slightly overlaying each other, resembling the shells which close the bodies of large terrestrial reptiles. . . . The steel plates were held together by thousands of rivets . . . .Fore and aft arose two cages with inclined sides partly closed by thick lenticular glasses; one destined for the steersman; the other containing a brilliant lantern to light the road. Midway of the hull was a platform surrounded by a rail whereon we stood, and which was reached by a stairway and an iron door."

Unlike Captain Nemo's *Nautilus*, my submarine could be controlled entirely by one man. By filling tanks with water it could be submerged. By emptying them it could be raised to the surface, and it could be steered to port or starboard or manœuvred generally by the single operator. Moreover, in addition to the air lock by which Captain Nemo and his men left the *Nautilus* to wander upon the floor of the ocean, my *Nautilus* was equipped with torpedo tubes.

The launching took place without a hitch and when everything was complete I invited the Governor of the Bahamas to be present at the tests. Accompanied by his A.D.C. and the Chief of Police, in full uniform and regalia, His Excellency inspected the boat. As I had

never put it to an actual test, I was not at all certain how this strange craft might behave. I knew it could be submerged, but I was not so confident that it could be raised to the surface with entire success at the first attempt. To keep the vessel on an even keel beneath the sea was one thing, but to gauge the ballast tanks to such a nicety that the vessel would bob to the surface right side up was another matter. All of this I explained to our distinguished guests.

Ordinarily I planned to handle the *Nautilus* myself, but on this occasion I trusted her to Jack Gardner, who was clad in a diving-suit as a precautionary measure. All was going well. Fascinated, the Governor and his party watched the shining hull as it broke through the surface like a mammoth whale. Off the riveted plates the sea water poured miniature cataracts. Up rose the railed platform, up came the rounded cigar-shaped hull. And then! Cries of dismay came from the spectators. Wildly the craft rolled. It heeled far to one side, in imminent danger of turning turtle and drowning the man within, who would be caught like a rat in a trap. My heart was in my mouth. My exhibition seemed about to end in tragedy. Everyone was excited and shouting. And then slowly, smoothly, the *Nautilus* rolled back and came to rest at an even keel.

I saw the Governor slap the Chief of Police on the back, and heard him exclaim: "By Jove, these motion picture fellows, you can't baffle them, you know."

"She was well over one hundred feet in length"
CAPTAIN NEMO'S "NAUTILUS" IN "20,000 LEAGUES UNDER THE SEA"

Chapter VIII

THE FIRST FILM DRAMA BENEATH THE SEA

AT last all seemed ready. We could now begin the actual filming of Jules Verne's marvellous tale. I had divers, diving suits, the rebuilt yacht, undersea guns, the submarine and the *Abraham Lincoln*. This old brig had been completely transformed. She had been re-rigged with the huge single topsails and heavy spars of a frigate of Civil War days. A funnel rose above her decks, along her sides were gun ports and on her deck she carried real guns.

I had gone over every scene in the story with the utmost care. I thought that everything needed for each scene was on hand, except one—and this one perhaps the punch of the whole film, the big smashing thrill of the entire drama: the desperate battle between divers and a giant octopus.

Herein lay my greatest problem. I could hire divers. I could build submarines. I could reconstruct vessels to conform to a period half a century earlier, but—how was I to procure a giant octopus to take part in the story? And even if I found one, should I be able to induce any of my divers to risk their lives in a hand-to-hand struggle with the monster? But I decided not to worry over the matter. Octopuses were in their dens among the coral reefs and the old wrecks of the West Indies. Somewhere, I hoped, my searchers would find a giant of his kind—the father of all octopuses, and it shouldn't be difficult to get him into the picture once he had been located if a diver could be induced to offer himself as bait. At any rate that particular scene could wait. We had plenty to occupy us for months ahead. By the time we were ready for the battle with the octopus, the problem might solve itself.

Accordingly, preparations were made to film the first episode in Jules Verne's tale, the ramming of the *Abraham Lincoln* by the *Nautilus*. It was not such smooth sailing as I had thought it would be. My *Nautilus* did not possess the great "iron spur" that Captain Nemo had provided on his submarine. He might ram a frigate with ease, "passing through it like a needle through sackcloth," but for me to drive my submarine into the hull of the tough old brig might result in the destruction of the undersea boat, with perhaps no great damage to the old-fashioned warship we were supposed to destroy.

No, we must manage to give the effect of ramming the ship without actually doing so. And now a new and unforeseen difficulty arose. Jules Verne wrote in describing the scene on the deck of the *Abraham Lincoln*, "A fearful shock followed, and, thrown over the rail without having time to stop myself, I fell into the sea."

A realistic description, for a vessel struck by Captain Nemo's steel-spurred submarine would surely receive a "fearful shock." She would heel far over, and if our picture was to be convincing, our *Abraham Lincoln* must also heel to the blow and register a "fearful shock." Just how to bring this about was a puzzle. Then, some brilliant genius in the company had an inspiration. He suggested that by placing water-filled barrels on the deck and rolling these in unison to one side of the ship at a given signal, she could be made to list heavily. This appeared to be a solution of the difficulty, and we decided to try it overnight. A local rum importer was found who was willing to loan us the necessary barrels. Laboriously they were placed on board. Fifty men sweated like navvies filling them with water dipped in bucketfuls from the sea. At last, weary, with aching backs and tired muscles, the men had filled them all and placed them on greased runways. Just then the owner of the barrels appeared, informing us that he had immediate need of them, and demanded their return at once. Our words might well have caused the paint on the *Abraham Lincoln* to shrivel and blister. But I had had about enough of the scheme. By now a survey of the whole plan had convinced me that it would not work. All of those thousands of gallons of water had to be emptied back into the sea and the empty barrels returned to their owner.

Again I read and re-read my copy of *Twenty Thousand*

Leagues Under the Sea, trying to find a way out. At last
I had it! In the story the frigate fired at the *Nautilus*
from a distance, the first shot missing the submarine
the second striking it, but glancing off. According to
the story, it was not until hours later when Ned Land
attempted to harpoon the supposed leviathan, that
Captain Nemo lost his patience and rammed the ship.
Here was my chance, my way out of the dilemma.
I would alter the original story to suit the exigencies
of the occasion. I would have the frigate fire at the
oncoming *Nautilus* at close range, and in the cloud of
powder smoke and the tense excitement of the scene,
no one would notice whether or not the *Abraham Lincoln*
registered a terrible shock and heeled over when
rammed by the *Nautilus*. And as Jules Verne stated that
the real *Nautilus* struck the frigate's rudder post, I could
by careful manœuvring and with good luck, run close
under the ship's counter and give the exact effect of
ramming without actually touching her at all. First,
however, I must provide for another detail of the scene
as described by Verne, for I was determined that our
picture was to agree with the story in every point as
far as was humanly possible. The story laid particular
stress on Ned Land and his attempt to harpoon the
Nautilus, thinking it was a whale. I determined to
duplicate that episode, but unfortunately, not a man in
the company had ever hurled a whaling harpoon. But
the actor who was playing the part of Ned Land

135

seemed, with his splendid physique, ideally fitted for the part. He had handled the harpoon for weeks without ever having practised throwing it. Yet it seemed a simple matter, merely to stand in the ship's forechains under the bowsprit, and when the undersea boat drew near, to hurl the weapon. But there was more to throwing a harpoon than the actor reckoned.

Jockeying the vessels into position as they surged through the open sea, I ran the *Nautilus* diagonally under the frigate's bows. Cameras clicked. The uniformed crew of the warship rushed excitedly forward and peered with amazed faces over the bulwarks. Then the impersonator of Verne's great character, Ned Land, raised his weapon and heaved it with all his strength. But he had forgotten a most important detail. He had failed to have the line which he was holding coiled, free to run with the harpoon. As the harpoon sped through the air, the rope whipped into a loop, wrapped about the actor's neck, and came within an ace of flinging him from his perch into the sea. But with the trick of cutting when it came to the editing of the film, we used only the first flash of the harpoon-throwing scene, then showed a close-up of the harpoon striking futilely against the steel hull of the *Nautilus*. It worked out perfectly. The actor's mishap was merely a humorous incident compared with what followed.

When my divers weren't busy diving, they worked

as actors in the above-sea scenes. And now I had Tuck and Gardner, both vitally important to my under-sea work, playing the parts of gunners on the deck of the frigate. They had had experience with the type of cannon to be fired at the submarine as she dashed at the frigate's stern.

We were ten miles out in the open ocean, and it was not easy to manœuvre the clumsy vessels owing to a stiff breeze which was blowing, but soon they closed in. The scene was an utter failure for I had passed well beyond the stern of the frigate in the submarine before the cannon fired. The gun, an old-fashioned muzzle-loading cannon, had not belched forth its charge when the gunner had touched it off. Thinking the priming had missed fire, Tuck and Gardner bent over the cannon, their faces close to the touch-hole, when with a roar, the charge exploded, back-firing into the faces of the two men. Blinded, burned, cursing with pain, they staggered back into the arms of the company doctor who providentially was on the job and on deck. In fact he was in Naval uniform and acting the part of the officer at the wheel. Rushing the injured men below deck, he packed their faces in cracked ice, and sitting on their chests, picked the burned powder grains from their frozen eyeballs and faces. But this was merely first aid. One of the men was in hospital for weeks, and to their dying days both will bear the marks of the unfortunate accident.

All of this was disheartening and discouraging, but the picture must go on. To add to our troubles, the triangular fins of sharks were cutting the water around the frigate. Scraps of food thrown overboard had attracted them. The actors who were to take the parts of Ned Land, Professor Arronax, and Conseil, flatly refused to throw themselves overboard as the story demanded. Nor could I blame them. Jules Verne makes no mention of man-eaters on hand, and sharks were not mentioned in the actors' contracts. Doubles had to be provided to act their parts in this phase of the scene. Even so, we were obliged to go through with the entire scene ten times, working from six o'clock in the morning until sunset before we got it right. But by this time, practice most certainly had made us perfect. The frigate's gun thundered as she stood silhouetted majestically against the low back-lighting of the tropical evening. I rushed the *Nautilus* at the ship's stern. Even Captain Nemo himself couldn't have done a better job. Here was realism with a vengeance, and in my anxiety to make the scene convincing, I overdid it a bit and actually knocked the massive rudder from the stern of the *Abraham Lincoln*.

After this I felt sure the acting and photographing of the divers hunting in the coral forests and the crew of the *Nautilus* wandering about the floor of the ocean and salvaging the golden bars from the wrecked galleons in Vigo Bay, would present only minor difficulties. Actually there was but one serious trouble. As we progressed with our undersea work, I discovered that the divers, stimulated by the effects of the chemicals they breathed, felt dreamily happy after being down three or four hours, and often, after playing their parts in a scene, they would wander away on excursions of their own, exploring coral caves or picking sea anemones and would be missing when we required them for the next scene. It was a curious experience to have these hardened veterans in this serious work go off picking flowers like children. It was also dangerous.

As I have already explained, the chemical oxylithe when exhausted affects the diver's brain like alcohol and constant care must be taken that the charges are renewed promptly every hour. On one occasion, working over-time in an emergency we came uncomfortably close to tragedy.

The divers had emerged from the air-lock of the *Nautilus* to the sea-floor, and had been working for a long time in a particularly thrilling scene. As they prepared to re-enter the submarine, they suddenly fell upon one another like maniacs, fighting desperately. Struggling, utterly crazed by the exhausted chemical, one of the men was caught in the current, swept off his feet, and knocking a valve which inflated his suit, was thrashing aimlessly toward the surface. Helpless, entirely out of his mind, I fear to think of the conse-quences had it not been for Biggie, a seven-foot giant

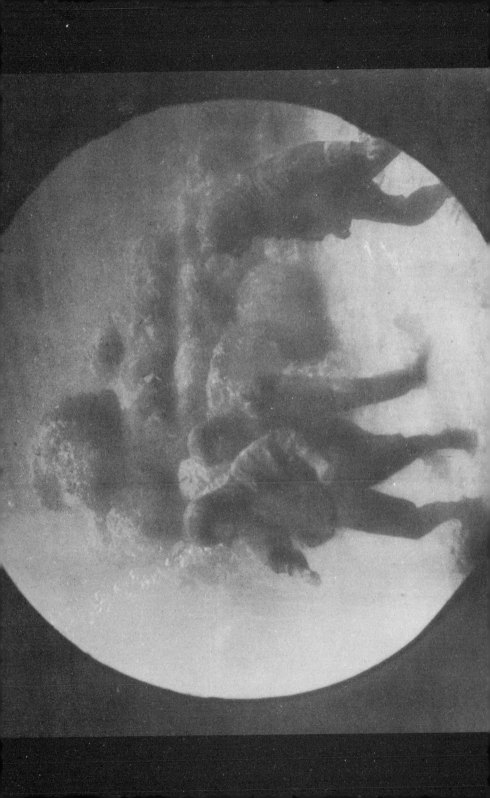

and one of my native Bahamas crew, who reached down from our diving boat as the diver swept by and grabbing him with one hand he landed him weights and all right on to our deck.

Had his rescue been delayed a moment longer he might have submerged again and been lost. Even as it was the diver's face was horribly black. He was foaming at the mouth. His finger-nails had dug deep into his flesh. It took five men to hold him down as he fought like a demon.

The diver in trouble was Crilley's brother. By this time Frank Crilley himself, who had been a party to the undersea mêlée, had reached the deck. Obviously he too was suffering from the intoxicating effects of oxylithe. Still dressed in his diving-suit, he sprang forward with doubled fists.

"I'll fix him," he cried. "All he wants is a crack on the jaw. Let me give it to him. He'll dream his way out of it." We held him back with difficulty. His brother was slowly responding to treatment.

But Crilley was not as crazy as he seemed. A crack on the jaw had been used before in such circumstances with stunning success.

Day by day, week by week, the reels of the exposed film increased. Thousands of feet had been shot. We were in the middle of the picture when one Sunday morning fire broke out on one of our vessels. A coloured boy had left a four-gallon tin of petrol on the

"They would wander away on excursions of their own"
DIVERS IN SELF-CONTAINED HELMETS

galley-stove after using it to light the fire. Our boats were moored together in the harbour and the flames soon spread, burning furiously and destroying everything to the water's edge except such boats as we were able to scuttle. When at last it was over, only the charred hulks of our vessels remained above the cinder-littered sea. Practically everything had been destroyed, including nine self-contained diving-suits.

Fortunately the holocaust was not as disastrous as it might have been, for while I had not foreseen a fire, I had provided against losses by possible hurricanes and had a full equipment in reserve. This saved the day. The burned vessels were salvaged and repaired. Three weeks from the time of the fire we were back on location and the undersea cameras were grinding away once more.

Now came preparations for taking the strangest, most striking and impressive picture I have ever made beneath the sea—the burial of one of the crew of the *Nautilus* on the bottom of the ocean. Let me quote from Jules Verne's account of this intensely dramatic scene:

"Captain Nemo had stopped. I saw his men were forming a semi-circle around their chief. I observed that four of them carried on their shoulders an object of an oblong shape. We occupied the centre of a vast glade surrounded by the lofty foliage of the submarine forest. Our lamps threw over the place a sort of clear

143

twilight that singularly elongated the shadows on the bottom. At the end of the glade, the darkness increased, and was only relieved by sparks reflected by the points of coral. On observing the ground I saw that it was raised in certain places by slight excrescences with lime deposits, and disposed with a regularity that betrayed the hand of man. In the midst of the glade, on a pedestal of rocks roughly piled up stood a cross of coral that extended its long arms that one might have thought were made of petrified wood. Upon a sign from Captain Nemo, one of his men advanced; and at some feet from the cross, he began to dig a hole with a pickaxe.

"I understood it all! This glade beneath the sea was a cemetery, this hole a tomb, this oblong object the body of the man who had died in the night after the mysterious battle. The captain and his men had come to bury their comrade in this resting place at the bottom of the inaccessible ocean! The fish fled on all sides while their retreat was being thus disturbed. The hole was soon large enough and deep enough to receive the body. The bearers approached. The body enveloped in a tissue of white byssus, was lowered into the grave. Captain Nemo with his arms crossed upon his breast, and all the friends of him who had loved them, knelt in prayer."

I determined that this scene should be a masterpiece. But there were great difficulties to be overcome. I could not reconstruct the scene in precise details. If my divers dug a grave in the ocean's floor, as described in the story, they would stir up ooze and marl, blotting out everything and making photography impossible,

I should have to alter this detail and have my men inter the body of their comrade in a natural undersea tomb, a coral grotto. Otherwise the burial scene should be exactly as Jules Verne had pictured it.

Days were spent in preparations and rehearsals. More days were spent searching for just the proper setting, in trying to locate a suitable cavern in the heart of a coral reef. Patience and perseverance had their reward. We found exactly the right spot; and as I watched from my undersea chamber and saw the procession of weird, grotesque figures moving slowly along the ocean's floor with that ominous, shrouded form, I actually felt awed and impressed with the solemnity of the occasion. Reverently the burden was lowered and placed within the grotto. Masses of limestone were lifted and set in place, sealing the mouth of that solitary tomb beneath the sea. The uncouth figures knelt and above their heads rose the cross in its pristine purity of snow-white coral.

With bent heads and slow steps the men turned away. One by one they passed from view, leaving the glade deserted—deserted save for the bright-hued, inquisitive fishes that swam dreamily about the arms of the lonely cross.

Chapter IX

MISHAPS AND ADVENTURES

ONLY three really big scenes remained to be filmed; the torpedoing of the yacht, the ascent of the balloon which was to carry the Jules Verne characters to the mysterious island, and finally, the undersea battle with an octopus.

This battle would be truly a daring undertaking, and, if anything went wrong, it might mean an "undertaking" in more ways than one. However, the giant creature was yet to be located, so while the search continued I decided that next in order was the sinking of the yacht.

There would be no doubt as to the full destruction of the craft. Explosive experts on the staff would see to that. They would arrange the explosion so as to create a most effective picture. This must be done in the open sea, and the submarine *Nautilus* must appear as the avenger. We were going to photograph the explosion as the torpedo from the *Nautilus* struck her, show timbers and débris hurtling through the air, picture the roaring flames sweeping over the yacht as she sank lower and lower, plunging at last beneath the sea.

147

When the yacht sailed to her doom, trimmed for action, she would carry a cargo of enough dynamite, black powder and petrol to blow up a battleship. Everything must go like clockwork, for this was a scene that could not be retaken. We had one chance and only one, to get a successful picture. More than $25,000 was to go up in flames and smoke. We couldn't afford to fail. Every detail, every act, every movement of every participant, whether actor or crew member, must be timed to a split second.

The entire scene was gone over with the staff, the crew and the actors. Hammered into their minds was the importance of concerted action and following the schedule to the letter, so there could be no mistakes, no slip-ups, nothing to prevent the scene from clicking perfectly.

The plan was as follows: the yacht was to be placed near some rocks that jutted out of the ocean, and on which the camera men were to be stationed. At a given signal, which was to be two pistol shots, the men on board the yacht were to touch off the time fuse on the explosives, and dash away to safety in their motor-boats, while the *Nautilus* was to run into the scene in order to save the hero and heroine, who were to leap from the doomed yacht into the sea, and be picked up by Captain Nemo and his crew.

Of course, everybody and his neighbour's wife in the port of Nassau had heard of the spectacle about to be staged, and hundreds of pleasure craft had put to sea that day, and gathered about us at a safe distance, that is, as close as possible without being in the actual scene itself. Steaming into the foreground was the Governor's launch, with His Excellency, his wife and a party on board, the Governor having accepted our invitation to be present on this occasion.

It looked like a gala day. Everything was going along splendidly. Unless something entirely unforeseen occurred, this scene could not fail to be a smashing success. The camera men were in their places on the rocks with their cameras focussed on the doomed yacht. The avenging *Nautilus* was manœuvring for position. All ears were attuned to catch the sound of the two shots from the signal man's pistol. That signal was vital, for it would set all in motion. Hundreds of yards of open sea, splashing about in a brisk wind, separated the groups awaiting these two shots.

Below deck in the submarine I was talking to some of the actors.

Suddenly from the direction of the rocks came the report of a pistol shot! I sprang to my feet. It could not be the pre-arranged signal—the allotted moment had not arrived. The *Nautilus* was far from the yacht, while the Governor's launch was within a few dozen yards of it. But the men who were to touch off the explosives had been warned to act on the instant. At the crack of the pistol, they leaped to their task, never waiting for the second shot, and by the time I reached the deck they were dashing away in their motor-boat. The explosion was coming! I held my breath. The Governor of the Bahamas was well within the danger zone. He was standing there with his wife and party on the bridge of his launch, looking at the yacht, not knowing it would explode in their faces at any moment; and to add to my horror the launch, Governor and all, must surely be in the picture.

A volcano seemed to burst into eruption. Flames, smoke, shattered planking and timbers were flung high in the air! Débris showered about the Governor's vessel. Then I jumped into action. Somebody had made a mistake, but it was too late to do anything about it. Out there on the water, $25,000 worth of yacht was going up in fire and smoke. Her bow was sticking up in the air—in a moment she would sink!

I headed the *Nautilus* into the scene toward the blazing remains of the yacht. Slowly we neared the projecting bow. Every effort was made to clear it, but the current was sweeping us so close that the actors on the deck of the *Nautilus* could have reached out and touched the bow of the sinking yacht with their hands. I was just below them in the open hatch, safely out of range of the grinding cameras. The scene on the *Nautilus* was impressive, regardless of the catastrophe. Captain Nemo stood erect, formidable, arms folded across his chest, his revenge now complete. Tears

"A volcano seemed to burst into eruption"
THE EXPLOSION WHICH WAS ALMOST TRAGIC

streamed down the heroine's face as she went through the pantomime of thanking Captain Nemo for her rescue, but I could see from her trembling that her tears were not all acting. The hero, fully alive to the tenseness of the moment, was manfully acting his part.

Then suddenly I remembered—inside the yacht's bows were a thousand gallons of petrol that had not yet exploded. The light of the fuse might be creeping up to it now, for all I knew, though evidently something had mis-fired, to hold back the explosion until now.

But the petrol was there; fire and explosives all about it, ready to go off. I was terrified, faint and sick; almost paralysed with suspense, expecting each second that we should all be blown to atoms. Actually we hung under the bows of the burning vessel only a brief moment, but it seemed a lifetime. As far as the camera was concerned, this part of the scene was perfect, for, just as we passed the yacht, she slipped back into the sea, plunging to the green depths below.

It was over! There were cheers from the spectators. Their Governor was safe. Although timbers flew all about his party no one was injured. Again the onlookers cheered and cheered. Then boats scattered in every direction, homeward bound, or to fishing grounds or bathing beaches. It had been a great show! Soon the last of the pleasure craft disappeared into the distance.

A starlit night settled down on us before we had

assembled our men and equipment and started our trek back to the harbour at Nassau eight miles away.

As the fleet rolled along the blue-black sea, I lay flat on the deck of the *Nautilus*. I was completely exhausted, utterly discouraged. It was all painfully clear to me now. The end of the scene could be used, even as it went off loaded with death; but the beginning, the explosion on the yacht, a six-foot flash costing $5,000 a foot, would be a total waste if the Governor's launch appeared in the scene. And all because a fool assistant, wishing to make sure that the pistol was in working order, had fired a shot to test it.

And now the suspense! We would not dare develop this precious strip of film in the tropical heat of our testing laboratory at Nassau, served only by rainwater from the housetops. We must wait for the laboratories in New York to give us the result of the development. That was all that could be done about it. Wait. The camera men had been questioned. They did not know. Flying splinters from the explosion had reached them on the island. In the excitement of the moment, and not looking for the launch to be in the picture, they could not be sure about it. It might be in the picture— and it might not. All this uncertainty only added to the agony of suspense, growing through the days of waiting until the cable arrived from New York.

It read: "Launch not in picture." The scene was a knock-out! It was perfect!

With the successful culmination of this episode, we next turned to the balloon ascent. In the part of the story we were borrowing from Verne's *Mysterious Island*, the balloon starts from the square in Richmond, Virginia; and in Nassau's Ralston Square, facing the harbour, I saw the counterpart of the scene in Richmond, fifty years before. The colonial setting, the sun-drenched square, carriages and donkey-carts passing, picturesque darkies among the white citizens, all seemed to fit into the pattern—a flawless replica of Old Virginia. We did not have to be carried back there.

Just how we were to arrange for a balloon ascent in the busiest part of old Nassau without disrupting business, traffic, and the populace generally, was another matter. We conferred with the officials, the police, and the Governor, and came to an agreement that seemed satisfactory to all concerned. We were to have the square to ourselves at night, with the privilege of keeping the crowds at a respectful distance, and to do anything we pleased within reason, on the promise that the square should be cleared of all our props and possessions before morning, and that everything should be restored to its normal condition for the day life of the city.

We set to work that evening. The square was brilliantly illuminated by our batteries of powerful arc lights and flares. Our balloon was a hot-air affair, and so was the air of the town; that night it was stifling.

So to say that we worked feverishly would be no more than the literal truth. In order to fill our huge bag with heated air, it was necessary to provide a trench or pit in the ground, in which to build a huge fire.

The square had never before been dug up. It was of solid limestone. In fact, the lower parts of some of the buildings facing the square had been hewn out of the native rock. But there were grave-diggers who were artists at the work of carving into the limestone structure of the island with their gleaming axes. They were busy men, and much in demand, for when a person died in Nassau, he had to be buried the same day. Seldom was he interred more than a foot or so under the solid ground. So we hired grave-diggers, who dug like black demons. Spurred on by deep draughts of rum and their own weird incantations, they carved their way down into the white rock. It was a Herculean job, and long before it was finished, the pink blush of the eastern sky warned us that dawn was near. There was nothing to do now but fill up the hole, smooth it over, pack up and move bag and baggage from the square.

It was plain that if we were ever to get our balloon inflated, we would have to find some speedier method of digging the trench. There was but one solution— more grave-diggers! The second night came. Again our ghoulish labours commenced. The grave-diggers worked in relays, plying axe and shovel, but once more daylight found us quite unprepared to make the ascent.

Again the square had to be left smooth before the arrival of the first townspeople. By the third night our nocturnal operations were regarded as a form of local entertainment. By the fourth night the sporting element were laying bets as to whether or not we could get the trench completed, the fire going, and the balloon inflated before daybreak.

I began to feel something like a character in a fairy tale under the spell of a malicious necromancer, condemned to labour all night, only to see the results of my hard work vanish with the rising sun, bewitched into going on endlessly, for ever, and never getting any nearer to achievement.

The spell broke one night when the trench, having been dug and refilled so many times, was easily excavated, and was ready with a hot fire and the balloon in position by midnight.

By now our industry had been elevated from the plane of mere entertainment to the status of a social event. Each evening the people gathered about the square. As night advanced more and more onlookers would appear. After dinners and dances the élite of Nassau would make their appearance, gorgeous in their formal dress. Even when the sun was rising above the rim of the sea there would be a few night owls left to watch us "fold our tents like the Arabs and as silently steal away."

On this night word was passed that the balloon was

BRAIN CORAL
OUT OF WHICH IS GROWING A STINGING GORGONIA

positively going aloft. The little city was on tiptoe with interest and anticipation. It was like the announcement of a circus parade in a country town, the première of a feature film in Hollywood or the expected arrival of a trans-Atlantic flyer. It was a big event. To add to the commotion somebody with more imagination than brains, seeing our guy ropes attached to the base of the Victoria monument, had started the rumour that we planned to carry off the statue of the gracious queen with our balloon.

From far and near, from all parts of the island, people had flocked to the scene. The glow of our flares against the night could be seen for many miles. One excited darky exclaimed as he arrived panting that he had seen "a great light shinin' to the heavens."

Like moths attracted to a flame came the superstitious natives. They filled the grassy park which extended from the scene of our operations to the water front. As the nights of excitement continued many of the native black folk had camped about town with their women and children, living only for those glorious hours when the bright light would shine again. They arrived in donkey-carts, filled to overflowing with young and old. Negro dandies with their "gals," strutting about in the glory of flaming neckties, gaudy shirts and yellow-buttoned shoes, stumbled over fat black mammies nursing their piccaninnies. As time went on, weary with watching and "jes' natchally tired" hundreds slept on the grass in motley array. They looked like the dead on a battlefield.

The fire was roaring in the trench. Hot air and dense clouds of smoke were billowing into the balloon that was slowly expanding, taking form like a giant mushroom, filling the centre of the square. Excitement in the crowd rose to fever heat. There was another rumour abroad that we intended to blow a hole in the treasury which faced the square, and steal the money!

Our men were hurrying and working. But in spite of all we could do, the balloon seemed strangely loath to leave the earth. Dramatically posed in the balloon basket were four dummies, dressed in Civil War uniforms, representing the characters who were to escape from Richmond in the balloon. Yet there were no indications that the great bag was ready to soar up toward the brilliant tropical stars that spangled the velvety black sky above.

Perhaps our fire was not hot enough. The balloon man provided a brilliant idea—pour petrol into the trench. Intent only on getting our balloon up and taking the picture before daybreak, we watched him carry out his idea. Cautiously at first, then rapidly as he became bolder, he fed the explosive liquid to the fire. It was doing the trick! The monster bag stretched with a mighty heave, as though it had taken a deep breath. Then a roar and a flash! Like a titanic rocket, flaming and awesome, the balloon shot to the sky.

Hell broke loose. With one unearthly scream, the mob turned and dashed away. The strong trampled over the weak. All were in one mad rush to escape the huge ball of fire. Bony old carriage horses that had been fast asleep, their noses drooped to the ground, now reared straight up on their hind legs, turned in the air and galloped away like two-year-olds—but they were not running half as fast as most of the natives.

Others, frozen with terror, were in the grassy park kneeling in Al Jolson attitudes, "mammified." Some grovelled on the ground, digging for a hiding-place. And well they might, for up in the air was a burning mass; ropes, gear, and the great basket of the balloon. What goes up must come down, and somewhere that basket with its fiery occupants, was bound to hit—and it did—right in the middle of the park, missing by inches a huddle of terrified negroes. Preceding its arrival, one of the "passengers" of the balloon had descended from above, banging down beside a quivering mammy who was lying prostrate with her face buried in the grass. Brushing the arm of the uniformed officer from her neck, she took one look at his battered countenance, and with a leap, shouting, "Lor-r— Deliver me! Amen!" she jumped into the bay. A dozen or more followed her, for the corpse was smoking and the negro's fear of death in any form is appalling.

There were no casualties. Police dispersed the crowds, sending the stragglers home. The city scavenger did his work. With a small army of men and women sweepers, using brushes made of palm fronds, he directed the sweeping of the lawns and the brushing up of the entire square. Meantime we had made good our word and had moved off without leaving a trace. Every reminder of the holocaust that a few hours before had belched to the sky, was gone. The kindly face of Queen Victoria, carved from the white marble of her monument, looked down serenely on the customary life of the square. The long shadows of the morning faded away. It was another day.

Later, with a gas balloon and a make-believe Richmond, we obtained the scene in a studio lot. Yet even now old negroes in Nassau can be heard dating all births, deaths, and marriages from that night of nights "when de balloon burn up."

Chapter X

MAKING JULES VERNE'S DREAM COME TRUE

THE great day arrived for the battle with the giant
octopus, a natural climax to our thrilling undersea
adventure.

I knew where my octopus was lurking. The stage
was set. One of my most daring divers would take the
part of Captain Nemo. I was confident he would go
through with the scene successfully, but I was not so
sure of the native diver who was to take the part of the
pearl fisher. To assure realism I had had this man
agree to play the part, dive in and gather his pearls,
without his knowing exactly what was going to happen
to him. He knew that something unusual was up when
he saw several armoured divers sink silently down into
the sea, just outside the camera range. However, the
native had sublime confidence in me, and the promise
of a big bonus if he made good.

With the octopus, the pearl diver, and Captain
Nemo all at hand, we were ready to go. We were
prepared to undertake the filming of the most astounding and extraordinary scene ever attempted.

"What a scene," wrote Jules Verne in describing the harrowing experience of the pearl fisher. "The unhappy man seized by the great tentacle and fixed to the suckers was at the caprice of this enormous trunk. He rattled in his throat, he was stifled. The unfortunate man was lost! Who could rescue him from that powerful pressure. Captain Nemo rushed at the monster and with one blow of his axe cut through one arm. For an instant I thought the unhappy man was to be torn from the powerful suction of the tentacle. . . . Several of the eight arms had been cut off. But just as Captain Nemo and his men threw themselves on it, the monster ejected a stream of black liquid. . . . It seemed as though the slimy tentacles sprang up like hydra's heads. My bold companion was overturned by the tentacles he had not been able to avoid. Ah, how my heart beat with horror. The formidable beak was open above its victim. The unhappy man would be cut in two! I rushed to his succour. But Captain Nemo was before me. His axe was buried between the enormous jaws, and Ned Land plunged his harpoon deep into the triple heart of the creature."

What a picture!

As Jules Verne had placed the scene of the terrible battle with the octopus in the West Indies, it seemed something more than a coincidence that we should find ourselves in the same locality for our combat. An author, however, has one great advantage over a producer of motion pictures. He can imagine and describe a setting to suit his fancy or his needs. But in taking

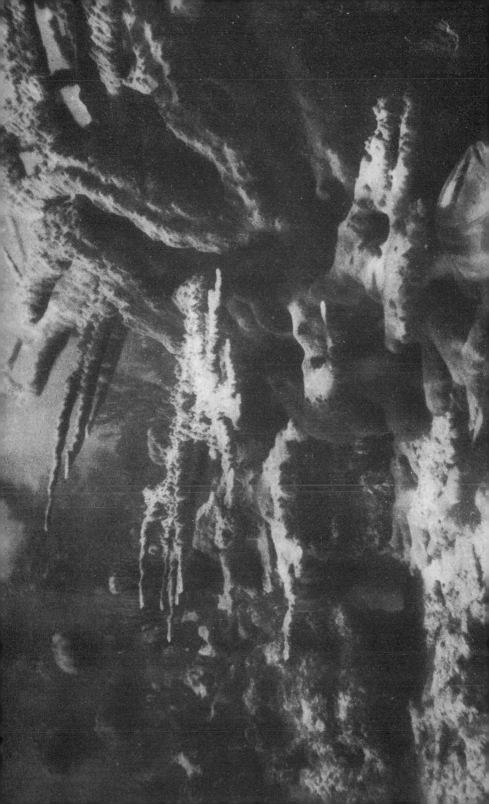

a motion picture, and especially one under the sea, the producer must operate in surroundings that actually exist. In this instance we were indeed fortunate. The spot where I expected to film the giant octopus might verily have inspired Verne's description of the reef where Captain Nemo rescued the pearl fisher. A rocky reef overgrown with marine life, with gigantic coral-trees whose roots formed dim mysterious grottoes and caverns, an eerie spot where the sinister shadows of great sharks moved menacingly through the undersea jungle; where huge morays twisted like giant serpents among the sea fans, where crabs lifted great claws and where, in any of the murky caverns, the huge loathsome octopus might lie in wait for its prey.

At any moment I expected it to appear as I sat at the controls in the photographic chamber, with my camera man at my side.

I could not but admire the daring of the native who was to act the part of the pearl fisher as I signalled him to stand by for his plunge into the water. A human bait for the monster octopus.

All was ready. The epochal undersea conflict was to begin! It was a moment of breath-taking suspense. Surrounded by a frame of gleaming silver bubbles, the native came plunging into view. With a few swift strokes he approached the coral reef, alert, eyes searching the caverns, the deep grottoes, the mysterious shadows. Tip-toeing crabs scuttled to their holes like ballet

"Where the huge, loathsome octopus might lie in wait"
A LOVELY SETTING FOR HORRIBLE TRAGEDY

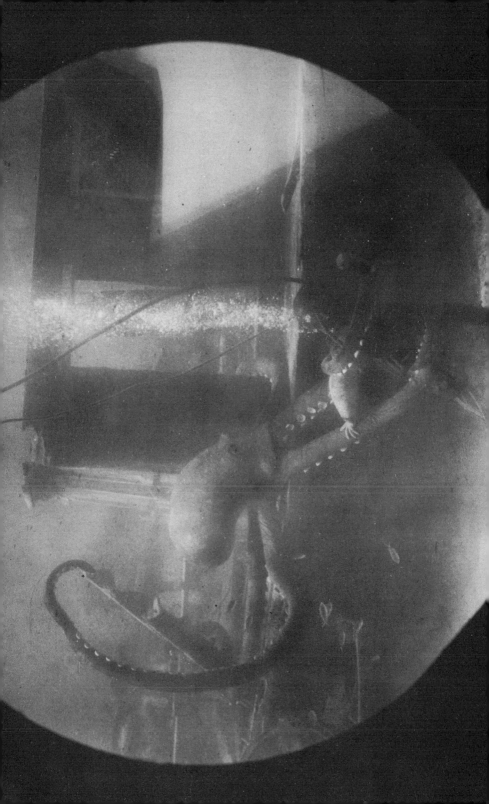

dancers vanishing into the wings of a stage. And then
—a shudder ran through me—I pressed my face close
to the glass, staring. I knew what to expect, I was
prepared for it, but the actual sight of that great pulpy
body, those great staring eyes, those snake-like sucker-
armed tentacles, sent a chill of horror down my spine.
The giant cuttle-fish glided with sinuous motion from
its lair. Loathsome, uncanny, monstrous, a very demon
of the deep, the octopus was a thing to inspire terror
in the stoutest heart. The native saw it. He turned—
struck out for the surface.

Too late! Like a striking serpent, one great writhing
tentacle shot out and threw a coil about the hapless
swimmer. Frantically he struggled, but the sinuous arm
of the octopus drew him down inexorably. Here was
stark realism! And all the while the clicking of the
camera told me that not one detail of the gruesome
scene was being missed.

How much longer could the native struggle there
beneath the sea? Bubbles of air were escaping through
his lips. Soon his lungs would be empty. Already, it
seemed, long minutes had passed since he was seen
swimming down from the surface in an aura of bubbles.

Into the field of vision came the grotesque figure of
the helmeted diver, the gallant Captain Nemo. How
slowly, how very deliberately he seemed to move.
Moments dragged in tense suspense. Now he was
beside the native who was struggling in the clutches

"The formidable beak was open above its victim"
WILLIAMSON'S OCTOPUS IN AN EXCITING BATTLE WITH A DIVER

of the squirming python-like tentacle. A flash of his broad-bladed axe—the tentacle fell—and the struggling native shot to the surface, gasping for breath but saved! A great cloud of ink gushed from the octopus, blackening the sea about the wounded monster, obscuring the courageous Captain Nemo, and through the murky screen I caught glimpses of the writhing, twisting tentacles, flashes of the axe, and the struggling, grotesque form. Elated, I yelled with joy. Suddenly a current swept the inky veil aside. With his body wrapped about by the clinging tentacles, Nemo was battling furiously, while beyond him, unspeakably horrid and menacing, were the great round staring eyes, the huge pinkish body. But one by one the gripping tentacles were relaxing their hold. The creature seemed ready to abandon the struggle. Another cloud of ink enshrouded the scene, and when the water cleared, Nemo was moving toward us, axe in hand.

The master scene was over.

With this epic battle on the ocean's floor filmed, my undersea work on *Twenty Thousand Leagues Under the Sea* was complete.

But the gods, in the shape of producer-distributors, who rule the destinies of motion pictures, must have their innings. To them a film with no studio or "lot" scenes was simply unthinkable. The fact that Jules Verne's story was laid almost entirely beneath the sea did not influence them in the least. Captain Nemo's adventures began with the story of the Sepoy Rebellion, therefore, argued the potentates there must be scenes of war. Accordingly, nearly $50,000 was added to the cost of the picture by staging a terrific battle. It was money thrown away. When shown on the screen the fight between soldiers on land seemed false and commonplace beside the undersea battles between men and monsters of the deep. Most of it was scrapped after the opinion of a famous newspaper critic was read: "If the rest of the picture were discarded, the undersea scenes alone would be worth three times the price of admission."

It seemed that we had timed our entrance into the picture-show world just right, for by the strangest coincidence, the picture opened the same day that a German U-boat suddenly appeared on the coast of the United States, electrifying the nation and monopolizing the headlines with the news that the elusive U-boat had slipped through all blockades, crossed the Atlantic Ocean, and had torpedoed and sunk half a dozen British ships just outside New York. Later the submarine slipped safely back to Germany.

To quote one of the leading Chicago papers: "If the Kaiser had been its press agent, *Twenty Thousand Leagues Under the Sea* could not have been timed to better advantage."

Chapter XI

A SKELETON IN MY CUPBOARD

I HAVE a secret to tell. It's the secret of the skeleton I've kept hidden in my cupboard for a long time. It is no mere human skeleton, for it has eight arms— long sinuous ones—that have helped to weave the tale told in the preceding chapter.

The terrifying octopus that chilled the blood of millions of movie fans in the thrill-creating battle-scenes, was one of my own making. To all observers, and even to myself, it appeared frightfully alive, and capable of performing the most devilish of octopus tricks. In fact it could and did perform them, bringing to the screen the ultimate in realism, and providing the punch to the picture version of Jules Verne's master-piece. But the octopus was my brain-child. It was not spawned in the open sea, but in a tumultuous sea of production details.

What was the visual result? Let me quote from the *Philadelphia Ledger*:

"What company has juxtaposed sharks, octopi and divers à-la-Williamson? The struggle between the monstrous cephalopod and the pearl diver, ending in the latter's rescue by the captain is one of the rarities of the camera. There can be no question of fake or deception. It is all there, and our vision tells us that it is all true. This one scene alone will give *Twenty Thousand Leagues Under the Sea* the acclaim by word of mouth that brings the dollars."

Such opinion by Press and public was universal. Acceptance of the scene by the movie-going public was of paramount importance. It was the desired goal, for I was in the business of providing entertainment, building up thrills for the movies. Such unstinted praise and full acceptance of the unique octopus scenes was my joyful reward for all of the ups and downs I had undergone in this business of thrills.

When Jules Verne's *Twenty Thousand Leagues Under the Sea* was first published, a great deal of it was supposed to be the wildest sort of fiction. The truth of the matter is, however, that practically all of it was based on scientific fact. Jules Verne was the first great writer to popularize science. While his writings may have seemed visionary to the public, the secret of his success lay in the fact that he was an expert at compiling data from the British Museum and other sources, and of weaving them into a highly dramatic story. By careful weighing of the known facts he built his story on a solid foundation of scientific truths. So when it came to producing his master story in films, I resorted to his method of rounding up scientific knowledge and especially facts which concerned the octopus. Octopuses up to a spread of twenty feet or so were well known to me, but I was determined to find one for my picture with a spread of at least thirty feet, and therein lay my great problem. From the first I harboured an idea in the back of my head that if I could not find this giant octopus I wanted in the sea, one as large as I knew to be fully recorded scientifically, I would find some way to re-create the dreaded monster and make it work for me.

Throughout all the complicated developments of the film, the eight writhing tentacles of the octopus were weaving about in my mind as the search for the real thing continued. And search we did—above and below the sea—for signs of such a giant cephalopod. But the deadline in production was drawing near and an octopus had to be forthcoming. I set to work and this is what I did.

I decided to model my creature after the octopus in the Brooklyn Museum, a marvellous reproduction made from measurements and details of a natural specimen. The giant tentacles could easily attain a spread of thirty feet or more.

First I produced one tentacle. It must writhe and squirm and reach out and take hold of objects, draw them in, coil round them like a python, to resemble in every detail the deadly arm of an octopus. I derived

172

the first idea of the tentacle movement from a familiar toy, a rolled-up paper tube containing a coiled spring. When this is put in the mouth like a pipe and blown into, it runs out in a straight line. When the air is released it coils back with a snap. That part of the movement seemed simple enough, for with huge tapered springs and other attachments, I could regulate and vary these movements of the tentacle.

Next I produced a tapered rubber tube, like the inner tube of a tyre, about sixteen feet long, with which to inflate the tentacle. As no human breath would be powerful enough to inflate this tube to a sufficiently high pressure, I resorted to compressed air. With springs, inner tubes and outer coverings to represent the skin, and with sucking-disks attached, I had a fairly representative tentacle of a giant octopus. At its extreme end it was about an inch and a half in diameter, and near the body where it was to join in with the head, it was over six inches in diameter. Hooking this up with high-pressure fittings I found I could shoot in the compressed air, straighten out the coil of the huge tapered spring and reproduce the movement of the octopus tentacle. But when I released the air and the inner tube became deflated, allowing the spring to coil back, the tentacle became a loose flabby thing, and wouldn't do at all. I had foreseen this difficulty, however, and had prepared a fine coil-spring to run the full length of the tentacle, running round and round, starting at the small

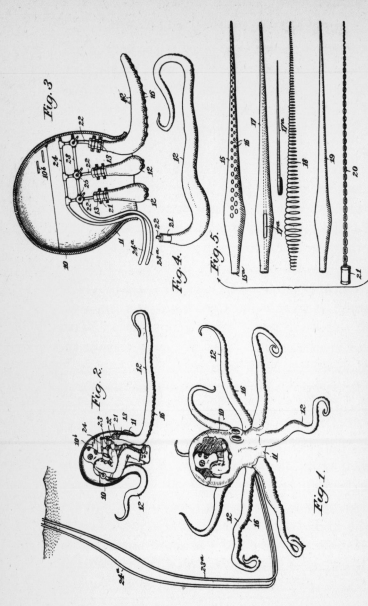

"I placed the controls inside the head of the octopus"
THE MECHANICS OF THE WILLIAMSON OCTOPUS

end and coiling up to the large end. The coils of this spring were but a fraction of an inch apart, so that when the inner tube deflated, this finely-coiled spring sustained the form of the tentacle. Now, whether deflated or inflated, I had what appeared to be the real article.

The problem of how to make the sucking-disks had exercised me considerably. As the tentacle tapered the sucking-disks were also graduated in size. What could I find that would simulate these disks and also stand the wear and tear of the terrific strain to which the tentacle would be subjected in its undersea battle? That seemed a real problem, but the answer proved to be simple. Rubber balls of graduated sizes were split in half and sewed to the skin of the tentacle. When mottled in its natural colours, the entire tentacle appeared life-like in every particular.

So far so good. The accompanying illustrations of the details will help to illuminate the points. But making one arm of the octopus was only one part of the devilish creature's make-up. All eight arms had to be considered collectively. How these were to be woven into the head in a natural and flexible manner, and how they were to be manipulated under the sea, I finally worked out. As the illustrations show, I placed the controls inside the head of the octopus, and to supply the creature with brains, I placed a diver, wearing a self-contained suit, inside the head as well. The duty of this diver was to put the octopus in motion and to convey to it my commands for the scenes in the film.

Eventually it worked like a charm. The effect of the octopus gliding with sinuous motions was startling, even to me, and to one who did not know its inner secrets, viewing it in action was indeed a hair-raising experience. If one snake shown on the screen can bring chills to an audience, eight serpents combined in the fiendish head of an octopus can multiply the thrills a thousandfold. John Barrymore himself told me that in all of his career on the stage and screen he had never been so thrilled, so absolutely frozen—rooted to the spot—as when he viewed the amazing spectacle of my octopus scenes in *Twenty Thousand Leagues Under the Sea*. What he wanted to know was how I did it. I told him I might tell him sometime. Here is my answer.

But let us delve a little deeper into the creation of this sea monster, the octopus. Admitted that I am not presenting the octopus in my scenes as a scientific display, and that I produced the octopus sequence in my film from the viewpoint of one in the show business; now let us see what the scientists do in their work in the great museums. Suppose, for instance, they want to show you a lion as in life and in its natural habitat. What do they do? First, with metal, wood and other materials, they build up a skeleton framework of the lion in action. The actual skin of the creature is pulled over the form and sewed up. Then with fur and mane carefully groomed, whiskers attached and a pair of perfect glass eyes, they present to you their king of beasts. You gaze at it in wonder. The perfection of the reproduction is startling. The thing seems to live and breathe. Now should the lion make a forward move, should it roar or suddenly charge at the behest of the scientists, would they be nature-fakers? Of course, I realize the accepted museum standards of exhibition and I know that scientists have no desire to turn a museum into a menagerie through manipulation; but where is the dividing-line where the faithful recreation of any animal produced for any desired effect should be considered the act of nature faking? And where the fake, if any?

But getting back to my giant octopus, I found that to produce its form and movements were not all. There were more intricate matters to be considered. The matters of water pressure and buoyancy were most difficult to deal with. When inflated, each arm of the octopus required about a hundred pounds of weight to neutralize it, so that the octopus would sink and become to all intents and purposes a part of the undersea world. How to distribute nearly half a ton of weight throughout its body and yet have it flexible and seem as light as a feather in the water was one of my most ticklish problems. The weight must be substantial yet almost fluid in effect. The fragile construction of the creature added to the difficulties. Getting it in and out of the sea

was another problem. Also, it took quite a few experiments before we could provide it with the means of executing its most spectacular function—the throwing of a great cloud of ink. First, I used a supply of writing-ink, and ran it through one of the tentacles into the body so that it could be released and expelled from the head in a natural manner. Gallons of this ink were used. It seemed to be doing the trick, but still it did not give quite the natural effect. It was too dark for octopus ink. One day I was discussing the need of a slimy sort of substance that would adhere to the body of the octopus, when one of my West Indian divers produced a quantity of sticky marl from a swamp. Dropping some of this marl into the sea, I noticed that it quickly dissolved and produced a perfect sepia ink. My ink problem was solved. A truck load of this marl was quickly obtained, diluted, and placed in great hogsheads from which, with force-pumps, I could furnish my octopus its ink supply. Finally I had it all tuned up to perfection. My creature could now move bodily about, throw its cloud of death, and shoot out its terrifying tentacles at will—my will.

In *King Kong*, a later startling film production, a man-made giant gorilla was the central figure. This amazing animal dominated practically every scene. It seemed to live and breathe and even to experience human emotions. Its movements were conceived and executed so realistically that the public accepted the

"The skeleton in my cupboard"
THE OCTOPUS AT REST, AFTER A HARD DAY'S WORK

existence of the creature as actual—at least for the hour they viewed the picture. What the public may have thought of it after the show affords food for conversation. The producers made no secret of the fact that the giant Kong was a mass of motors, a man-controlled mechanism. It is in this same category that my giant octopus must take its place. As in the case of Kong, it was entertainment that I was producing.

While necessity was surely the mother of this creature, and relatively speaking, I was its father, I must say I had a lively and thrilling time creating those eight giant arms, that ugly head and weird form, and in making the evil-looking creature get down to work and play its great and important rôle in the Jules Verne masterpiece.

Chapter XII

THE MYSTERIOUS ISLAND

HOLLYWOOD was my destination.
It was springtime, March 1st, and my army of ideas and hopes seemed to be marching along in fine formation. In my pocket was a contract stating that I was engaged, "tied up" with one of the greatest film-producing companies in the world, to co-direct a master film—one that stood to cost well over one million dollars. It was to be all in colour photography, a mighty production. And I had never been to Hollywood. Not that this apparent incongruity meant that I had been running the wrong way with the ball. As Kipling has indicated, there is an East and a West. That always applies, and the movie industry is no exception. There are studios in the East as well as in California. In the East I had had ten years as an independent producer, with approximately that many successful film productions to my credit. My offices were in New York, my studio the floor of the ocean in the West Indies. Yet the magic city, the Hollywood of 1925, was the mecca of all movie makers. And I was making my pilgrimage.

The catacombs of New York's Grand Central station were far behind me and the singing rails beneath my train were clicking the miles away when the conductor punched my long ribbon of ticket entitling me to the 3,000-mile ride and said with a quizzical smile, "Hollywood." And I wondered what Hollywood meant to him who had seen so many go out there—and come back.

What did Hollywood mean to the people I would pass on my journey—a million an hour—girls and boys of all ages, working in factories, behind counters, the vast public bound to their tasks, nourished with the thrills of the movies which carried them off to a world of make-believe?

I was engaged in a marvellous industry which thrived on their thirst for romance, one that filled them with delight as they made gods of the stars, lived their parts with them, learned all the details of their private lives, and fed on the gossip. I was going to the fountain-head of their dreams, to the cinema heaven of the legion of feminine charmers, young and old, the army of young men taking stock of their profiles, and the host of budding writers, all supremely confident that they could show up and outdo the established Hollywood régime. Yet I knew I was not on my way to any fantastic dream city such as existed in the imaginations of the vast public and readers of fan magazines. It was enough to be going to the real Hollywood; to be one of those on the inside, one of those who know by hard experience how far the amateur is wrong, yet who are conscious of the fact that from this outer sphere, ever presenting itself so surprisingly new, comes the material for the Hollywood of to-morrow.

Anyhow, I was getting a big kick out of my excursion into the West.

A cycle of ten years had passed since I had produced Jules Verne's *Twenty Thousand Leagues Under the Sea* and with a brand new audience grown up, the movie world was ready for another great undersea film. Jules Verne had written a companion story to his great masterpiece. We could merge the two under Verne's own title of the sequel, *The Mysterious Island*. With modern production aids and the magic of colour photography, a great caste of stars and players, my storehouse of under-sea experience, and all that Hollywood could supply, it seemed that we had all of the ingredients of a classic, with box office success assured.

There were to be many delays, however, and much time was to be spent before Verne's story could be made suitable for a "movie" success; for many weeks all minds focused on the epic battle to bring the "Island" up to date. Conferences bred more conferences, as each idea, launched in a breeze of enthusiasm came limping back to port with sails down. The flickering midnight oil might find one of these sessions in progress at the home of the great star already assigned to play the lead. And varying from the work-day hours on the lot, night conferences would often be held in my hotel room and elsewhere, and the supervisor once called a meeting for eight a.m. at his home—an unheard-of hour in Hollywood.

Finally, somewhere in the mist, a form seemed to be taking shape—a story—one that seemed to suit the studio heads. No incubator baby could have been nurtured with greater care than this effort which seemed to bring *The Mysterious Island* closer and closer to the camera lenses. But it developed very slowly, and with many setbacks.

Then, at long last, the modernized version of *The Mysterious Island* seemed to burst from its swaddling clothes. It grew to fantastic and amazing proportions. Instead of the truly romantic character that Verne had depicted, in the Civil War period, the now modern Nemo, central figure of the story, was monstrous. On an up-to-date island with the advantages of modern death-dealing science, if he ever wreaked the vengeance at his command, it would be so all-consuming and terrible that it would be a cataclysm for which no sane man could be responsible.

Then there followed a conference of the master minds out of which came the bright idea that if Nemo would not do these things while sane, then why not make him crazy? So poor Nemo went crazy and could now carry out any business that could be conceived for the picture. Then still another difficulty arose. With all these mighty and modern agencies of vengeance possible, and growing larger daily, the wrong for which Nemo sought revenge seemed too small, too insignificant, for such horrible reprisal. The injury he had suffered must be magnified. That was going to be a tough nut to crack, for he was already bearing up under the worst of hurts that should scorch a man's soul. Again the writing staff went into a series of confabulations. The next day came a call from the boss.

Seldom was anyone summoned to his inner sanctum. I had reached it only once in my lifetime. I was a moment late, for the call had been a hurried one and the lot spread out over fifty-three acres, but I hastened to the appointment. Maybe the boss was going to call the picture off. By this time I felt that that would be good news to me. As I entered the door the boss stopped short. He had started a speech to the ring of talent that surrounded him, filling every seat and space around the four walls of his office. Courteously, and in his customary low tone, his face pale and calm, he said, "Come in, Williamson. Have a seat. I want you to hear all of this." There was a ripple of a smile around the charmed circle for there was no chair left. But I quickly filled the gap by sitting on the upholstered arm of a chair already filled by somebody's bulk.

There was a moment's silence, then he began again, unfolding his plans to supply the missing idea, one that would give Captain Nemo the new and adequate motive for revenge. It would be a breach of ethics for me to repeat the idea he unfolded, but it was one where beauty and pathos were strangely blended, and through which the fascinating face of Nemo's wife appeared and reappeared with fleeting smiles of transcendent beauty. To me it was a story full of poignancy.

It held the entire crowd in its spell. There may have been yes-men in the room but there were also plenty of no-men, and no one said no. The boss smiled and relaxed for a moment. Yes, he believed that it was the big idea needed—a two-dollar idea. What he meant was a ten-shilling attraction at the box office.

Tackling his subject anew he went on dramatically, enlarging upon the plot for the picture. Now, with the motive for revenge supplied, he dwelt upon the new and modern Nemo. Here was this fiendish madman, a Jekyll and Hyde in character, supreme on his impregnable fortress, the mysterious island. This was his base of operations and at his command was every modern invention known to science: television, death rays and all the ghastly new devices for dealing out terrifying death. With full control of these forces above and below the sea he could wreck the world.

It was going to be a great picture and the conference was over.

The supervisor, with his staff of writers, left the lot to go off to the rarefied atmosphere of the Colorado

Mountains twelve hundred miles away, to think. It looked like fast action. Things were popping. After a time a wire came from Colorado as exhilarating as the climate up there. It said in brief, "We have it."

They brought it back to the studio, and when it was laid out on the table and dissected the story was impossible. It proved to be just another Hollywood corpse. However, in its short life it gained one distinction; it was the last of the modern versions of the book. A new supervisor had arrived on the lot and *The Mysterious Island* was the first thing handed to him on top of the heap of production he was to do—a prodigious load of work which he grasped most eagerly. He was young and could take it. And to top the excitement of his entrance into the arena, he produced a brand new idea, that the "Island" should be done in the actual Jules Verne period and not as a modern version! You might now think that we were back at our original starting-point, and that my scenario was to be used; but I was to learn by slow degrees that Jules Verne hadn't written a story big enough for this Hollywood lot. The powers had decided definitely they would not film his romantic adventure story, which my version followed closely. It must be something more than that, something much larger, something "*Big!*" And the Abraham Lincoln atmosphere with its Civil War characters was definitely "out." Richmond, Virginia was "out." For technical reasons

the story was now to be laid in Russia. Captain Nemo was to be a Russian, the whole cast Russians. These ethnological changes were satisfactory to me providing the story was right. The undersea possibilities were still open.

The supervisor said to me, "Now!—Where you have ten divers I want a hundred divers—two hundred if I can get them."—I knew that the profuse use of divers, like the profuse use of dollars, would not insure the success of this picture. The successful appeal of the film would depend on the carefully woven thread of human emotions running through it. If this were weak or broken, the picture, no matter how big it was made, would be but a robot, a Frankenstein, all show and spectacle, monstrous, but without a heart.

But it wasn't for me to halt expansion, and I could not pose as an oracle, for no one really knows—in pictures. If the picture were overbuilt, it could be cut, scissored to success. I knew by experience that both fortunes and faces had been tossed on the cutting-room floor.

Twenty-one weeks after I had thrashed everything out with the supervisor, Hollywood ordained I was ready to leave. The story had been gone over, item by item, and the continuity written. Everything had been mapped out and blue-printed to the last dot. I had selected my staff of assistants and others, and had carefully chosen the actors who were to double for the stars

'CINDERELLA" EXPLORING
IN A DIM LAND WHERE THE TREES ARE TURNED TO STONE

in the West Indies. They were to come on later. I was ready to go.

On my way out I stopped to say good-bye to one of the owners of the great company, the big boss of the boss.

"What!" he exclaimed. "Leaving? Stop! Hold everything!"

And so everything was held up for ten long days, more than trying to me, for another May and June had passed along with more ideal weather for my work undersea. Now it was July and hot. But I waited while every department on the lot went over the cost charts and blue prints, plucking $1,000 here, $500 here and $250 somewhere else, effecting a saving in production, still on paper, of about $75,000

Then after a final warning on cost from the boss, oddly coupled with the pronouncement that even with the trimming the picture had just received, the company was starting the most expensively budgeted picture they had ever made, including "Ben Hur," it was decreed I could go.

This time there were no good-byes. Just a wave of the hand, so-long and good luck.

We were off.

Chapter XIII

THE MILLION-DOLLAR MYSTERY

TEN days of terrific heat in New York found me with my staff, and the tons of diving-suits, materials and equipment peculiar to my work, fully assembled, and on board the steamer, heading south. Gentle winds and a calm sea seemed to be paving the way to success. And, thank God, I could have three days' rest.

One night we beheld the rare phenomenon of a night rainbow arching through the bewitching scene of moonlight over the open sea. Jet black clouds were cutting across the heavens. It was a sign of a disturbed atmosphere, but it was hard to believe that anything could be ahead of us except the perfect weather we were going through. But a sudden lurch of the steamer told me we were entering a storm area. That evening I chanced to observe another bad omen—the captain hurriedly leaving the wireless room, with trembling hands. Investigating, I learned that a hurricane was moving up. We were in for it. All the next day we wallowed through the storm and that night we rode it out. The captain manœuvred his ship as if she were a living thing, taking the great waves first on the port, then on the starboard bow; but occasionally the labouring ship would drop into a great trough as if into an empty tub, and the next instant would be smothered from stem to stern with the hissing, seething waters. That night we received a crisp wireless message from the Nassau station. "Centre of tropical disturbance of hurricane intensity heading north-west over city within an hour." That was all. Not another sound came from the station. Its great wireless towers had been blown flat.

Next morning we steamed into the harbour. The wrath of the hurricane had been spent. All was hushed and calm. Sixty-five persons had been drowned in the Bahamas. Bodies floated in the harbour. My island base at Nassau looked as if it might have been pushed up out of the sea. Most of my fleet had been sunk. The vessel, *Jules Verne*, equipped with the Williamson Tube had foundered on a mudbank after another big vessel, broken loose in the storm, had swept it away from its moorings. The hatches were blown off, and inside, our vital machinery was coated with a half-inch of grey mud. Not a pleasant sight, especially when I recalled the loss of months of perfect weather through the Hollywood delay.

My small army of divers were as much at home under the water as above, and merely being swamped was but a ripple in the day's work. We soon overcame our difficulties, repairing all damage done by the hurricane.

During a previous scientific expedition I had explored hundreds of miles of undersea forests and had picked the choicest of these locations for the filming of *The Mysterious Island*. I established our main work base near Highbourn Cay, some forty-five miles from Nassau. Here a low-lying group of reefs or cays formed an atoll with the suggestion of a harbour at one end of the lagoon, although the highest elevation of any of the reefs was a dozen or so feet above the water.

With my previous experience in colour photography under the sea, the results were immediately successful. Exquisite scenes in colour came reeling in from the undersea realm. In addition to a host of native divers, I had my company of armoured divers, including such veterans as Crilley and Gardner. On the shore of the lagoon I was carrying out an odd piece of business, putting the diving-suits on dummies and arranging them in various groupings, so that I could illustrate to my divers just what they were to do when they were on their own in the depths.

Soon I was ready for the work of the stars, and needed the doubles I had selected, one of whom was Peggy Fortune, an aquatic wonder, who was to double for Sally O'Neil, who was playing the chief female part in the land scenes. I wired to the production head in Hollywood to send them on. A wire was back in an hour, "Exhaust all possibilities of finding doubles in Florida." This *might* mean that something had gone

193

wrong and that those I had selected were unavailable, but I guessed that it was a production idea of economy. It was only a dash across the gulf to Florida and I landed there early next morning. At Miami we flashed a hurried call along the coast and started the round-up.

At the Roney Plaza pool I started my survey with my busy assistant, Charley Stallings, lining up the prospects. There were humorous aspects to the experience but it was serious business to me. Not one was suitable. We made a hasty dash up to Palm Beach. The plan was to come back down the coast by degrees and see all. Palm Beach produced nothing. Neither did the towns just south, and we continued on to Hollywood—Hollywood, Florida. There by the sea I heard of a girl who seemed to have the appearance and the measurements required. But when I saw her, I knew instantly that she wouldn't do. The requirements were exacting. The first one was a natural similarity in poise and appearance to the star, and there were others. The over-developed shoulder muscles of professional swimmers were an immediate bar. I needed a slip of a girl who had everything—exceptional ability to swim and dive, plus beauty and the pliancy of youth. Above all she must be professional in recognizing the need to go and to do as told, with no mamma to guide her.

But this aspirant was charming; it was hard to say no.

She was eager for a chance so we rushed to the pool at the beach hotel. It was empty. They were cleaning it out. We were jumping into our car when the girl begged for a chance to go through her stunts in a pool at the Deauville casino some miles down the road in the direction we were going. I couldn't object, so behind our speeding roadster struggled a Ford filled with the ambitious beauty and members of her family who were in on the conference and probably hoping to be in on the contract, if any.

Again a drought. The Deauville pool was as dry as Sahara, with the high combing surf of the Atlantic ocean a stone's throw away. By this time I was convinced that doubles in Florida were definitely a wash-out. Night was coming on as we hustled away. There was quite a stretch between us and our starting-point in Miami and we were burning up the road. A rattle in the rear informed us that the unbaptized beauty was still with us. With the spirit of Ben Hur, she won by a nose as we reached the pool at the Roney. And there in the cool twilight, for in fact it was a tropical night, she sported in the water, eager for our approval. I had to summon all the graces of the art of refusal, learned through years with the movies, to say no—
—with thanks. By that time Stallings had California on the 'phone. I reported the exhaustion of all possibilities and of my own patience as well, and asked for my doubles. They were on the train next morning.

Ten days later, crouched in my undersea photosphere with my camera man beside me, I was directing an exquisite scene at the bottom of the sea.

Half buried in an undersea jungle, the rotting hulk and timbers of an old galleon seemed to harbour its priceless treasures of the past, and, spiralling down in a stream of bubbles into this eerie setting, came our sea-nymph, Peggy Fortune, doubling for the star. The technicolour camera was recording the scene with all its gorgeous colourings. Yet the menace of the wild ocean and its denizens was present and evident. Beauty and the beasts were there. A thousand forms of sea-life were about her. There was positive danger. But from both above and below, at lest six pairs of eyes were watching for her safety as she gracefully accomplished her difficult scene.

Nearly five fathoms down she had stopped by a huge "brain coral," to feed from her hand the voracious wild fish of the depths. She could easily do two minutes under water, astounding us all and especially the native divers, for she could outdo any of them in the art of which they considered themselves masters.

I assigned two men to the job of looking after her safety while sne was in the water, Bob Zimmerman, a giant of a man and a remarkable swimmer, and Cinderella, the pick of my native divers.

The tests of this scene were perfect as far as the action was concerned, but we found to our consternation that

197

"She had stopped by a huge brain coral"
THE "MERMAID" WHO PLAYED THE LEAD IN "THE MYSTERIOUS ISLAND"

we had a red-headed woman, a flame-capped mermaid, in our picture. This would never do, for the star in the studio for whom Peggy was doubling, appeared with soft auburn hair, and as the cuts were immediate, —going from the double to the star and back in an instant—the colour must match exactly. It was a trick of the undersea lighting that had distorted the colour of her hair, and a mad scramble was made for a wig. The one we finally used was a ghastly thing of strawberry blonde, but when filmed under the water a perfect match for the auburn tresses of the star.

With the new wig in hand there was a rush again to the undersea filming. My well-trained crew could fall in like a company of soldiers, and soon Peggy Fortune was re-enacting her scene, while flat on their stomachs on the diving platform with water glasses at their eyes were Zimmerman and Cinderella, ready for any threat of danger. Peggy had continued with her scene to the limit of her endurance, when the black boy above, with a guttural yell and a splash, shot down to the rescue. He thought he had seen a big moray too near to the girl. I stopped the scene. It was ruined for the picture, but I might have saved it for the comedy of that faithful old gorilla, Cinderella, pawing his signals to Peggy and chasing her madly back up to the surface. I immediately put in an order that no one was to go after Peggy until I said so; I would be the judge of the danger, and the scene was started again.

This time when Peggy passed close to an aged iron lantern projecting from the stern of the galleon, the trailing wig caught in the whorls of the lamp, scalping her perfectly, though she did not realize it, and went right on with her scene. I watched that precious wig breathlessly. It hung by a hair and might at any instant go whirling away in the swift ocean current. "Shall I get her, shall I get her?" shouted Zimmerman. "Hell, no," I yelled, "get the wig."

The scene was taken successfully a few minutes later, and we moved on to the next one.

With fifty people in my company the problem of living conditions on a coral reef had to be met, and I had a camp erected at the head of the lagoon. A most important factor was the cooking and eating. Dining upon the reef was in sharp contrast to the comforts of Hollywood. Of course, we had the very best food available, the pick of two continents, but it came to us in tins. At the back of the cook-house where old Pete, the cook, concocted his culinary wonders, a jagged mountain of tins began to grow to amazing proportions. With its peak glittering in the sunlight, it was a daily feature of interest to the restless members of the company. First in fun and then in fact, our habitat became known as Camp Kanopener.

While there was scant bird or animal life on the islands, the reefs on which we lived were infested with iguanas—huge lizards with jagged spinal adornments, scaly and sinister, with long black claws and a prehensile tail ever curved for flight or defence. They varied in size from little fellows not more than twelve inches long to grotesque creatures, measuring more than four feet, hideous to behold.

These reefs were honeycombed with holes, some of the erosions being as large as small caves. And in these cavernous depths the iguanas lived. But the savoury odours from our kitchen were a disturbing element in their lives, and even in broad daylight, without the cloak of night, an army of these creatures could be seen at all times, their beady eyes peering, as they moved down in rank and file to the cook's back door. The younger ones grew bold enough to venture into the kitchen and around under the stove, but as they got larger, a natural instinct warned them to retreat. About the cook-house door they gathered in companies, becoming larger in size with each succeeding rank, until from the underbrush in the rear leered the oldest and largest iguanas, red scaly pouches hanging from their throats. Suddenly a small one would grab a morsel of food and run, but it would seldom get far before the food was grabbed by a larger fellow, and so on down the line.

The cook had a method of trapping these animals with mosquito netting. The instant the net dropped over them they would turn over on their backs like a cat, and fighting with their claws, would become hopelessly ensnared. The cook, without scientific motive, began collecting. A local market boomed for these creatures as souvenirs, and boxes filled with them were soon sitting about the camp, each labelled as to ownership.

My best colour camera man grew weary of tinned food. He had visions of steaks and strawberry shortcake and ice-cream. Finally he refused food altogether and really seemed to be ill. Coming back from his work one day, the cook invited him in.

"I got something good for you to-day," he said.

The camera man sat down and sniffed delightedly at the steaming bowl set before him. He noted the pieces of flaky white meat floating about.

"Chicken soup!" he exclaimed.

"Yes, suh," answered old Pete, shuffling off. "Sit down and eat yo' fill."

This he did, enjoying every mouthful, saying he hadn't tasted anything to equal it in years.

"But where did you get the chicken?" he asked when there was no more soup in the bowl.

"Island is full of 'em," answered Pete. "There's one now." He pointed to an iguana scuttling by.

The camera man wouldn't believe it. His face turned a sickly grey-green.

"You're kidding me," he said stoutly.

But the cook took the unhappy boy down to the dump pile on the shore and there on the white sand showed him the claws and the head of the iguana.

The veil of decency must be drawn over the remainder of the session between the camera man and the cook.

The new moon had just started to wane. It marked the passing of the second month of our activities on location. The weather had been a bit "rugged" as the natives called it, but reasonably calm, and we had been getting along with our schedule. Yet the sunsets began to look queer. There was a coppery film over the sun.

One night the atmospheric silence was ominous. Uneasiness among the people increased with the buzz of mosquitoes and the torturing sting of sand-flies. Stallings came out to my flagboat where I slept on deck and asked me if I would come ashore. "I wish you would help me to hold them," he said. "They're getting hysterical." The monotony and the strain of it all was worrying even the best of my company ashore. I hustled to the camp willingly and made use of an old scheme my father had told me he always practised at sea—getting all hands busy at something. There was an old guitar at the camp and soon everybody was singing the songs they liked best. Stallings hammered out a staccato obligato on his typewriter as he compiled a list of the favourite tunes which I made him paste on to the back of the guitar for future use.

At daybreak next morning the supply boat brought a gale warning. Two "twisters" were developing between us and the Caribbean Sea. One had been located, but the other was eluding the weather hounds.

Reports of it were vague. Its direction and intensity were unknown, but feared.

As I was just leaving camp for our location some two miles away, I stuffed the report into the pocket of my shirt. The curve of these storms is varied, and I could only hope we were out of their paths. In the lee of big Highbourne Cay, which was densely overgrown with low jungle, I hastily boarded the *Jules Verne* and began my work, inspecting the crew of nine men; then I went on to the smaller vessel, the *Enia*, a low, stout sloop with a long open cabin. This was my floating office and laboratory. Here my camera men were preparing for the day, and I gave orders all round to snap into action. We were all too busy to think about a storm, especially when there were scant signs of one on the horizon. We had taken our blow for the season, and were resting assured that the worst was over. The conclusion was reasonable for I had worked ten years in these islands without the interruption of a single hurricane.

We were steaming out from the half-moon bay in Highbourne Cay when a sharp blow sprang up out of the north. If this were going to continue it would interfere seriously with our work, so we swung back and anchored. Such a wind from this quarter was unusual and seemed ominous. We stood by watching developments, and by noon we realized that we were in for a gale. The direction of the wind was steadily shifting and through the scuds of rain and the foam of the sea it looked as though a hurricane might develop any minute. In all our equipment on the *Enia* I could find no barometer. One should have been hanging in its accustomed place, but later I discovered that one of my native boat crew, nervous about hurricanes, had borrowed it. Watching the action of the *Jules Verne's* crew some few hundred yards away across the stormy bay, I saw all hands working like mad to get out the hurricane anchors. They were running a network of long lines in every direction. By now I didn't need a barometer. I could smell a hurricane.

Everything possible had to be done to prepare for the worst. Manœuvring about, I let go all anchors on the *Enia*, and dropped back to get the benefit of the full length of the lines. By three o'clock in the afternoon a full gale was upon us and the crescent bay topped by the frowning jungle of Highbourne Cay was a seething cauldron. Out in the maze of white water mixed with the fierce deluge of rain, the *Jules Verne* wallowed in the sea. There was something most unusual happening aboard her. Through the driving scud I could see the nine men of her crew hastily leaping into the big long boat. The next instant they had cast off and had vanished like a streak into the murk. What did this mean? Had the vessel sprung a leak? Only some such peril or their barometer falling to the bottom of its scale could have frightened them into

deserting the ship. I hoped they would make land safely, but I knew they were taking a desperate chance. With the wind going around the compass, they couldn't be certain where the shore lay, for it had been lost to our vision for hours. On calm days nothing could be more lovely and inviting than the strip of curving beach on which they hoped to land; but on either side of this smooth coral strand arose the talon-like claws of the eroded coral reefs. If the long boat dashed against these it would mean torn bodies and possible death to some of the crew.

The sudden deserting of the *Jules Verne* by her crew caused consternation. Such a thing had never happened before and without a barometer we could only guess the reason for such a desperate move. On the *Enia* with me were my two best camera men, as well as Zimmerman and a weather-beaten negro assistant. In the midst of the terrific storm such things as the colour filters for the cameras had to be nursed, and like a hen about to be driven from her nest, these camera men were worrying about keeping moisture out of the colour filters. Like eggs in an incubator, these filters had to be kept at a certain temperature and, to keep out dampness, a lighted lamp always burned under them when they were not in use. The film for the cameras was nursed in an ice-box. Even that had to be maintained at a certain temperature. These were just some of the minute problems that were keeping

207

the men busy, while around them the immensity of a hurricane was building.

But the moment was to come when every man thought only of his life. There was positive alarm. I could see it in their eyes. The crew of the *Jules Verne* scudding for the shore had made them panicky. With the powerful Zimmerman as a guiding star, they had made up their minds to take a wild chance and swim for it, to try to make the shore as the others had done. But I would not permit it, and I warned them that they were being fooled into thinking that the will-o'-the-wisp shore was where they had last seen it. If we foundered, then we could all swim for it with our chances as good as now. We settled down to wait.

By now it was blowing a real hurricane, by far the worst of the six I had experienced. It seemed impossible that our little vessel could live through it. Everything movable that could be destroyed on deck had been blown away. Even the tightly-furled sails had gone. The devilish fingers of the gale had ripped apart the lashings and like grey ghosts the torn and tattered canvas had vanished into the blackness of the storm, leaving only the bare and naked spars, while a single strand of jib was all that remained, a pennant streaming from the masthead as hard and stiff as iron and screaming to the lashing of the wind. From every side, from the storm-tossed seas and the thrashing, flattened jungles of the hilly cay came a thunderous roar—waves of sound rising and falling, surpassing the mighty volume of a thousand symphony orchestras; yet through it all, like the shrill top note of a piccolo I could hear the high-pitched scream of that fragment of the jib changing in tone as it frayed away. God! If the thing would only break off and stop! That night I learned the real meaning of "the screech of a hurricane."

It was the long arm of coincidence that reminded me of the fact that only eight weeks before, while in the grip of the previous hurricane, two native sloops had anchored in the very spot where we were now. When the fury of the storm was over, dead bodies were strewn around the deserted shore for days, until by chance a government boat, searching among the islands, had found them, tragic, gruesome skeletons. A deep pit was dug near the shore and the remains of the bodies were rolled into it. I had actually seen the mound of new earth and the fringe of wreckage around the bay. Domestic articles of every kind, even baby shoes matted in the sand, and debris on the shore were pathetic evidence of the tragedy.

Were we destined to meet the same fate? Would our battered bodies be found stretched lifeless, rotting in the sun when the hurricane had passed?

Throbbing through my brain were disquieting, torturing thoughts of the camp on the low reefs of the lagoon. My people were there. What if the sea rose and engulfed them? Isolated in our storm-tossed vessel, we could know nothing of what was taking place on shore. The reefs, even the cay itself, might be completely submerged and everyone drowned without our knowledge. As that night of terror wore on, my thoughts wandered. Was this to be the end, the end of everything? I recalled those trying months of waiting in far-off Hollywood. Had all that delay, all of those disappointments, been merely a prelude to shipwreck, to death and the loss of my company on the jagged coral fangs? I felt personally responsible for them all, for I had brought them here—brought them here only to perish. And I shuddered as I thought of their friends, their families and their relatives. Who would tell them the tragic, awful news?

It was midnight when my gloomy forebodings were suddenly interrupted and I snapped back to reality and action. One of our anchor lines had parted. Two other lines held, but to prevent them from chafing away like the first one, I decided they must be attended to, or at any instant we might find ourselves entirely adrift. The storm was now at the height of its fury with visibility reduced to a few feet. I had heard of 100-mile an hour gales where one had to crawl along on one's stomach to keep from being blown away, or dashed away by the terrific weight of water accompanying the wind; but I had never experienced the thrill of a personal encounter with these elements in full fury until I went out on deck that night. My camera men had volunteered to help me do the job on the ropes, but I selected Zimmerman and the hardy coloured boy. Now we were inching along the deck while the wind, like a living thing, seemed to clutch us, to drag at us with irresistible force. Finally, through thundering waves and howling winds, we got to the anchor lines. Swinging out over the bow, I tried to shout orders, but it wouldn't work. The wind blew my mouth out of shape so that words wouldn't form, although with the bedlam around me a human voice meant nothing. So I resorted to pantomime and we were soon organized at the lines, wrapping them around with canvas and burlap to stop the chafing. Then we let go and with one slippery slide, we landed back in the cabin. My skin was burning from the force of the torturing pin-like blast of rain. I had gone out dressed in my underclothes, but as I stood in the light of the swinging lantern upon my return to the cabin, I realized my hurricane garments were gone—blown to a September Morn. It had been a strenuous battle, but now we felt more secure, and one by one the men succumbed to drowsiness, while the storm was still howling furiously. Zimmerman was shivering, so I covered him with a soaking wet mattress, and he too eased off to sleep. But there was none of it for me.

Like pendulums on the ends of our long anchor cables, the two vessels were swinging in the storm and occasionally I could see the bulk of the *Jules Verne* loom near our sloop. All moorings were in confusion for now we were pulling on our anchors in almost the opposite direction from what we were when the storm started. Again and again, through the milky scud of rain and sea the dark bulk of the *Jules Verne* would ride dangerously close to our sloop. There were two alternatives, either someone would have to swim to the *Jules Verne*, let go the anchor-line that was pulling it close to us or, as the vessels came together, we could jump for it. It would be a wild leap to try to land on the deck of the *Jules Verne* and broken legs or arms might result, yet it might be the one way out, for if the boats collided, ours, being the frailer of the two, would be the first to sink. However, I decided on the first plan, and awoke Zimmerman, and with the aid of the coloured boy we got to the deck again after I had fastened all of the available small rope to him for a life-line. Now he was ready to go. With the coil of rope in my hands I watched for the ominous bulk of the *Jules Verne* to come near again. Zimmerman was gone. Only a master swimmer could have lived through that turmoil, and soon Zimmerman was lost to me completely except for the feel on the rope as I let it run out. Soon I got to the last few feet. If he went much farther I would have to begin pulling him back. By now the vessels had swung far apart. He might miss making it. I didn't dare pull him back. The rope became taut and I leaned far over the side, hung on to the last inch, with Zimmerman tugging like mad. Then the strain eased. He had just caught hold of the stern of the *Jules Verne*. I waited, and as the vessels veered near again, I could dimly see him making his way along the deck. The anchor line he was searching for was now thumping up under our hull like a steel cable, but he let it run, and jumped back into the boiling sea.

I had some fast work to do now. Before Zimmerman had left us, I had asked him to dive and loop a hawser under the menacing anchor line from the *Verne*, and the moment he let go of it, with the help of the native boy, I whipped it up on deck and made two turns and a half hitch around our own mast. I wasn't letting go of any anchor lines in that storm. Then I had time to attend to Zimmerman. He was out on the end of that line somewhere. He had boasted of being at home in the water and that night he got his chance to prove it. I rushed to his life-line which I had securely fastened, and hauling in the slack we soon brought in Zimmerman, who was thrashing away with the Australian crawl. We pulled him aboard, but he didn't realize until the next day that he had fractured two ribs on that round trip across the seething gulf that separated the two boats.

Something like daylight finally arrived. Dying, the storm was almost as trying as when at its height.

Fumbling for something to write on, I found the forgotten weather report in my shirt pocket, now wet and soggy, and made a few notes on the back of it.

At last, the wind died down and the light increased until we could see the outlines of the desolate shore.

Squatting in a dismal row near the remains of the shattered long boat was the crew of the *Jules Verne* looking out at their vessel, still afloat on the now tranquil bay. Later I heard their story. Waist deep in the rushing waters they had clung to the small palmetto trees and somehow had gone through that terrible night. One of the coloured crew, a stuttering 250 pound giant named McGregor, had cried out in the night, "Goo-Goo-Goo-Good Lord, I'm going.—De whole earth sinkin'." These hardy natives had weathered fierce storms before, but this one was heart-breaking, killing. The captain of the boat, one of the finest men I have ever known, died later, a broken man.

Aside from minor damage to decks and rigging, our vessels and equipment were not hurt in the least. Even the light was still burning under the colour filters. The camera men had nursed this delicate mechanism throughout the storm.

An hour later I was at the lagoon a mile and a half distant, heavy-hearted. As I approached I saw the camp had been swept entirely away. Only a few figures moved about. Fearfully, I ran up the beach to investigate. Meeting one of the fellows—I couldn't

THE AUTHOR DESCENDING THE TUBE
WITH HIS LITTLE DAUGHTER, "CAPTAIN" SYLVIA

tell who it was for his body and face were matted with the sticky sand—I asked for the others. In a dazed manner he waved his hand toward the holes and the caves. There I found them, stunned and half stupid. When the camp had blown away they had run for the holes and had fought the iguanas for possession of this, the only refuge. It had been a fight for existence, too awful to contemplate. I started to check up and see if they were all there. Only one was missing, the girl Peggy. She was nowhere to be seen. I ran over the low ridge to the back of the reef. Glittering in the sand I saw the tangled strings and keys of the guitar. Gone was the box with the list of old songs. Nearby in the wreckage was a piece of a door with a lock on it. There was only one lock on the island—on Peggy's cabin. God! If anything had happened to that girl, I——

I looked up and from behind the jagged ledge of a coral rock came Peggy, smiling, radiant. After that night of wet hell, she had just been taking a swim. Now everyone was accounted for. I took her hand, and in her twinkling Irish eyes I saw that she caught the significance of my greeting when I said:

"Good morning, Miss Fortune."

No one had been lost, and except for their battering, our fleet of vessels in the lagoon was safe. But how would Hollywood re-act to this? I hated to think of it. As for food and supplies, there were none. Luckily our flagboat with its heroic crew was still available and I was making ready to return to Nassau over the milk-white sea, dotted with floating wreckage, when a rescue boat came up from Nassau to look for us. It was a big stout ship and I was glad to see it, and leaving a skeleton crew in charge, I took all hands down to our main headquarters for a change of clothing and a bath, to come back refreshed and ready to proceed with the work. At Nassau the awful news came over the wire. The storm had gone on to the Florida coast and had almost wrecked the city of Miami. Ships had been swept far up on the mainland and hundreds of lives lost in the Everglades section.

And together with news of the frightful disaster, I found in my mail an account of a Hollywood hurricane on *The Mysterious Island*. The first three reels of the portion of the picture that was being filmed in the studio had been re-shot and still the supervisor was not satisfied. The director, a Frenchman, despairing of ever being able to suit the supervisor, had given up in disgust and left for his home in Paris. Even though I lacked the details, I knew it had been a tempest that had rivalled in intensity the one that we had just been through. Now a new director who hailed from Denmark was assigned to the studio half of *The Mysterious Island*.

After an exchange of wires with the studio heads it was decided that we should rebuild and go on. This I did on the definite understanding that none of my crew or company was to mention the word hurricane, or anything in any way pertaining to it. By now the hellish noise, if not the fear of it, was gone, and even the smell of it, a very potent factor, had left our nostrils. Surely the tropical demons of Nature must be satisfied after dealing out two such terrific blasts. Within ten days the fluid dust from the bottom of the sea, composed of dissolved white marl, had settled. The water was as clear as crystal, like the great blue bowl of the sky above. And once more we were filming our scenes.

Meantime we rushed through the work of rebuilding the camp, this time much more substantially than before, using less canvas and more wood. Although it was a makeshift, the main building was quite habitable. Peggy was given a brand new cabin with quarters for her maid, and with the aid of an army of Nassau carpenters and native help we were soon in full swing again. One of our doubles, having nothing to do in his leisure hours, jokingly chalked up the hurricanes, painting them in black on the side of the building.

"Hurricane No. 1, Sunday, July 25th.
Hurricane No. 2, Friday, September 24th."

And then, to extend his humour, he added:

"Hurricane No. 3——"

218

This was supposed to be funny. No one had ever heard of three in a row.

And yet when the next full moon arrived in all its resplendent glory, the inevitable signs appeared again. We were in for another hurricane. For this one we were prepared. Unless there was to be a tidal wave, causing a great rise of the sea that would carry us off the island, I had figured we could weather it out, and I gave orders to stick to our guns. The entire fleet was anchored securely in the lagoon and as the storm increased and the night came on, most of the crew came ashore to take refuge in the main camp building.

I saw the way to utilize this man power and also the lumber supply outside and I got the men busy. Combining the tricks of seamanship and the art of carpentering, I had them lace and interlace planking across the framework inside the building. Great timbers were brought in to brace the walls. It was an ungainly looking job, but most effective. Crowding into the building with the crews came the Nassau carpenters, with their big straw hats still on their heads.

It was going to be a long wait, and packed into this one building everyone was using every ounce of weight and strength he possessed to keep himself and the building from being blown into the sea. It was stifling hot, for every opening was closed to the elements. Blasts of the storm would all but tear the building away, then would die down, only to come on again with renewed fury. Peggy had been provided with a cot which was under the dining-room table. She was fast asleep and her black maid stretched out on a plank beside her was snoring. I looked at the huddle of humanity about me. The whole scene was strangely illuminated by the glow of a few smoking lanterns which added to the stifling heat. Suddenly I realized how weary I was of it all.

The noise was terrific. The wind screeched like a maniac. Every crack and crevice served as a siren and the rain pelted upon the walls like the staccato reports of a machine-gun.

Then I began to hear strange new sounds. Over and above the roar of the hurricane with its fiendish crescendoes, I heard voices. Was I going to crack up? Was I going mad? They were human voices. I could swear to it. Men, women, even children were crying. I grabbed hold of Stallings and asked him if he could hear anything. Yes, he could. They were human voices—we were both sure of it—growing in volume, moaning and screaming. It all sounded unearthly.

Suddenly the canvas portion of the building bulged in and a face was thrust through a slit. What a face! I'll never forget it. It was that of an old darkey medicine man. The story the battered old countenance told in an instant was one of fear, pain, torture—hopelessness. I soon found out the reason, for as we jumped up and pulled the fellow in, he fell exhausted, and a stream of men, women, and children, with babies, pigs, and chickens, came tumbling after him. Some were crying, others were laughing, a curious trait of the negro, who can produce a primitive laugh when it's time for white folks' tears. Soon I was to realize that I was the host, and that we had guests from a shipwreck. Lost in the hurricane, these poor souls had scudded across the sea, finally to splinter their vessel on our shores, but thankful to God that they had found land. Seeing the dull glow of light in our building they had crawled along the reefs until they had reached it.

We did what we could for them. Soon the mothers were nursing their young. The pigs and chickens had been segregated. Most prominent of all in the confusion was one shapely young coloured girl who had hurt her knee. That injured knee became of paramount importance to the whole motley crew of the shipwreck. There was a howling demand for it to be cared for. In my bag I carried a bottle of liniment for a metatarsal weakness I suffered in one of my feet and my liniment was handed over. They poured it on in profusion until the pain in the injured knee was relieved. Presently I found myself becoming dizzy owing to the heat and the combined odours of the mass of humanity. We were almost stifling. Something had to be done.

I conferred with the old medicine man. He agreed that with the first lull of the storm he could take some of his hardier men and go elsewhere. I mentioned the caves, but not the iguanas. He said he had dragged a mainsail ashore and could take about half of his crowd and get out before morning. In the next lull he went. There was a general sigh of relief. But the next thing we heard was an ungodly yell and they all came back into the tent again. They had seen ghosts! Creatures were after them! What had happened was that in crawling up into the underbrush they had met the nine or ten dummies we had used in rehearsing our diving scenes, and running into cold outstretched arms had been too much. They were in again, all but the old medicine man. When daylight came I found him rolled up in his mainsail like a silkworm in a cocoon.

The flagship arrived with supplies and mail before sundown the next day. Again we had lost nothing but time, and when the water cleared we were ready to proceed. We were fast nearing the end of our new scheduled list of scenes. This time I couldn't help what Hollywood thought of it. I would see this thing through no matter what happened.

And then came news of the strange coincidence that was to round off the making of *The Mysterious Island*. In the batch of mail I received from the States was a bulky package. It proved to be a voluminous manuscript, a new version of the story. The director who had succeeded the great Frenchman had re-made the first three reels in perfect style and tempo to suit the supervisor. There were loud cheers. But it was the director's turn now. He didn't like the rest of the story. There was another pitched battle. Another terrific disturbance of positive hurricane intensity. The eminent director walked out. Back to his home in Denmark. He was through.

We were now matched in stormy blasts. Hollywood and the Bahamas, three each. Mine might be termed Acts of God, but the studio storms seemed somehow to lack divine dispensation.

A few weeks later I had shot all the remaining scenes. Now it was our turn to go home. Studio and Bahamas negatives were cached, put on the shelf to cool, and perhaps to solidify. Then a doctor was called, a reel film surgeon, for a major operation was necessary. Once more the story was rewritten, the main part of the picture recast, miles of it shot and reshot in the studio, sending the cost sheet creeping toward the second quarter million.

At last it was finished. It was heading for Broadway and the great public's approval, when a strange voice was heard—a voice that was heard around the world. It has never died down, for its echo was destined to go on growing in volume. It was Al Jolson's voice in the movies. Sound had arrived! And instead of a great super-spectacle, our picture was a hushed and silent spectre.

Chapter XIV

SHARKS

A MILE deep, the Tongue of the Ocean between Andros and the New Providence Islands of the Bahamas forms a popular hunting-ground for sharks and game fishes in this part of the West Indies. Here I descended beneath the sea through the Williamson tube, determined to enter into the private life of the man-eating shark. I had prepared a feast in anticipation of him divulging his innermost actions and habits, good and bad. I seemed unwelcome at first, for in the eerie depths, as I cruised through the corals fringing the ocean wall, the absence of sharks caused me some concern; but after I had dumped overboard some fifty gallons of animal blood I was suddenly welcomed by these wolves of the sea with an enthusiasm bordering on madness.

Out of the soft blue haze loomed a pack of the largest sharks I have ever seen. Well in advance came a huge Hammerhead shark, setting the pace to reach the bait. Looking up from below I could see that the cloud of blood was descending, bringing closer and closer this company of frenzied demons which nothing

225

"Determined to enter into the private life of the shark . . ."
THE TIGER OF THE DEEP IN HIS NATIVE HAUNTS

human could withstand. Soon they were all around me, flashing ravenous looks as they passed. I studied them eagerly as, crouched close to my five-foot window, I gazed in amazement. Evidently the submarine cocktail of blood which I had provided had merely whetted their appetites and obviously the sharks were hungry for the meat course I personally represented.

Singly and in pairs they came head on, right at me, bumping their snouts against the invisible barrier that kept us apart. Would my glass withstand a blow from the Hammerhead? I could see it menacingly near with its thirteen-foot body of rippling muscles and a gleam in its wide-set eyes that startled me.

For the first time I saw in the eyes of the sharks before me a glow of warmth, a passionate look, not of affection for me, but evidence of the killing urge that was driving them to attack. In all my thrilling experiences among deepsea creatures, I have never before felt so crowded. My three-ton observation chamber was actually being jostled. I was rooted to the spot, spell-bound, while watching the mad dance of the demons. Attuned to the ordinary noises about me, I suddenly became aware of a strange new sound playing on my ear drums, rasping and chilling, like the croaking of a giant frog accompanied by grinding of teeth. Searching for its source, I found that a few inches away from me one of the heaviest of the sharks had started to chew his way in!

I drew back to watch its bulging eyes staring at me.
A glance along the massive body revealed a heavy mot-
tling of hunger blotches, adding terrifying meaning to
the uncanny sound that was echoing through my
metal stronghold—the crunching of the shark's saw-
like incisors around the edge of my window.

I had signalled to my crew above to lower down a
heavy baited hook. Its entrance on the scene immediately turned the tide of events, as the shark that took
the hook was pounced upon by the others. The sting
of their teeth drove the captive to frenzy and, ripping
free from the hook, it dashed off badly wounded with
the pack close behind. That was the last I saw of them.

That night our vessel was anchored out on the blue-
black edge of the tongue of the ocean. After a hard
day's work in the region of the sharks, my men were
resting about the deck and down in the open hold.
In view of my plans to demonstrate that sharks will
attack a man, I desired more evidence to prove my
case. In my past work I had had one or two native
Bahama divers who would drive a knife into a shark,
and among my present crew I felt sure of being able
to persuade at least one of the splendid diving boys to
carry out my experiment, provided there was a margin
of safety to himself. The fact that I must be behind
the camera necessitated someone else's doing the outside
work with the shark.

I soon found that super-salesmanship was going to be

necessary to make any impression; the courage of these men had been considerably shattered by hurricanes and some harrowing experiences in the previous months. Most of the crew were from Andros Island, where a vessel had recently been wrecked, and some of them swore as eye witnesses that many of the victims had been devoured by sharks. However, I began to offer inducements, money in increasing amounts, and then various articles I knew the crew coveted. Finally I caught sight of Ward, one of my new star divers, and recalled seeing him fondly gazing upon my dress clothes one night when he had rendered some valet service. Ward was about to get married. So I shot an arrow into the air. I offered to give my full-dress suit to any man who would take his knife in hand and attack a shark. Ward was nibbling at the bait. Then I added to the full-dress suit the further inducement of the starched white shirt and the patent leather shoes. Ward was hooked. His ebony countenance shone with anticipation. In imagination I am sure he saw himself dolled up in that dress-suit and I was perfectly willing, even anxious, to see him so adorned. Now he was willing to go the limit in the shark fight; he asked only one thing more, a wing collar, which I gladly promised to donate.

"Just think," I remarked with earnest enthusiasm, "for one short minute's work you will get a hundred dollar full-dress suit complete."

228

"I have found the shark to be a cunning, shifty antagonist"
A MAN-EATER HOOKED, BUT NOT YET CONQUERED

Then up from the depths of the hold came a funereal voice, "Yes, Ward goin' fight dat shark, goin' get dat suit, and life in everlasting."

I did not want to lose the ground I had gained, and to keep the men buoyed up I remarked, "Well, if none of you fellows will pull this stunt off the way I want it, I'll do as I did some years ago; I'll get my old shark knife, dive down and do the job myself."

Again the same voice came up from below, but now in a tone of total despair:

"Boss goin' get his knife—goin' fight dat shark—and then—what we goin' tell de Missus?"

Eventually the scheme was abandoned.

In all, I have found the shark to be a cunning, shifty antagonist against whom I am tempted to offer some words of warning. While there is hardly one chance in a million that you may need to recall my advice, I suggest that if you ever find yourself overboard with a shark coming for you, don't "Keep cool." Get busy! Kick up! Splash! This action may help, for a shark is generally cautious in attack and will likely turn away for a while before returning. Moreover, by no means take the immediate presence of a shark lightly, and feel safe because the upright dorsal fin indicates that the shark has not turned over, for I can assure you that a shark does not have to turn over to bite. It can close its teeth into a mouthful of anything without turning over one degree.

"I can assure you that a shark does not have to turn over to bite'

The theory that because of the position of its mouth the shark must turn over to get into action is erroneous. I saw a shark head straight for a diver without turning over, during my filming of *Twenty Thousand Leagues Under the Sea*. Equipped with a self-contained diving-suit this diver was hunting with a companion in the coral forests along the sea-floor. Sharks were plentiful, for we were baiting them into our scenes, and it had been understood before the divers went down that if sharks attacked, the men should stand back to back with their knives and guns in readiness, and release streams of air bubbles from their compressed-air tanks, a means of frightening them off—it had worked once before.

From my chamber below I sat observing the hunt in the mysterious setting of coral, when a big bull shark swung into action by circling around the divers. Back to back they crouched as the shark headed toward one of the men as if to bite at his head or shoulders. Impact with this huge onrushing body would easily have bowled over both divers. I was witnessing a rare demonstration of aqua-technique, for the threatened diver gripped the butt of his rifle to his side, and met the under tip of the shark's nose with the barrel as it rushed at him. Then, rising with all his strength, he shoved the head of the man-eater up, hurtling the grey body over his shoulder. With his head encased in a copper hood providing little more than a peep-hole

232

to see through, it is not strange that the other diver, with his back to the scene, knew nothing about the thrill his quick-thinking companion had experienced, or how near he had been to actual contact with the monster.

At the surface I have seen sharks repeatedly attack without turning over to bite. Once, with a slaughtered bull for bait, I watched a shark, swimming in normal position with dorsal fin upright, cut away a huge hip steak and dash off, still on the level, with the tail of the bull waving from the side of its mouth.

The porpoise-like roll of the shark as it comes to the surface, exposing an eye and the side of its white belly, may have given rise to the theory that it must turn over to bite, although the main reason for the manœuvre is to raise an eye above water in order to take an observation.

Sharks will fight with unbounded fury for food. I recall two that thrust their heads over the gunwale of a boat to get at a chunk of meat that had been snatched away from them in the sea. Side by side they pressed forward, snapping their teeth as we beat them with wood and iron. Finally, one of my men used an axe, chopping viciously at their heads, and reluctantly they retreated.

A sea captain recounted an incident to me which illustrates the voraciousness of the shark. One day, in a calm sea, with his vessel casting a deep shadow on the surface, he noticed the dark form of a shark lying in wait alongside. Then a man going forward threw a shadow on the water, and, like a flash, the shark darted out, snapping at the moving image.

An eye-witness told me of an accident on shipboard which cast a live man into the sea in a tropical port infested with sharks. The greedy killers crowded in on him so fiercely that he was pushed up from the water, and was seen to jump from nose to nose of the demons before he slipped and was lost.

Entering the reef area off Andros Island one evening in a twenty-five-foot motor boat, I was seated near Dr. Roy W. Miner of the American Museum of Natural History when a tremendous thump under the stern of the boat seemed to indicate that we had struck a reef, though deep water surrounded us. We jumped to the stern to look and there in our wake we saw a full-grown shark rolling over and over and bleeding from a gash across its throat. Evidently the shark had taken the underside of our boat for a speeding fish and had risen from the depths to drive its teeth into the planking near our propeller. Our engine was stopped by the impact as the whirling blades cut into its throat. The shaft was bent and the stuffing box broken, ending the usefulness of the motor boat for some time.

While the shark seems willing to bite into anything that looks like food, it can be particular at times. I recall one incident when such nicety was displayed.

While cleaning the outside of my observation window, well below the sea, a native Bahaman diver was surprised to see a shark reflected in the glass and right behind him. He dodged behind the metal chamber making quick time to the surface on a winding course around the tube. I had witnessed his hasty exit and the reason for it. The shark did not, however, follow him, but was attracted to the wad of absorbent cotton the boy had used for cleaning the glass. Expanded, the cotton was drifting away with the current, when the shark hungrily took it into its mouth, only to expel it at once. Apparently the lack of appropriate taste or smell must have been detected instantly by this particular shark.

Another time I noticed that sharks can be finicky was when they refused to devour a fellow-member of their family which we had caught and brought alongside. I could not fathom this, but later I got a clue when chancing to look into the capacious mouth of the captured shark. Squirming out of the white-roofed mouth was a vicious-looking black worm, and seizing it, I discovered that another one followed. Later I found evidence that his whole carcass was infested with these black boring worms, which undoubtedly led to the taboo by his comrades. However, the amazing and often gruesome variety of objects found from time to time in sharks' stomachs confirms the fact that they are indiscriminate scavengers of the sea.

I once found a four-foot barracuda intact inside a shark, thus settling the question of supremacy between these two rivals in at least one instance. Another time when off the Bahamas a shark was caught and hauled to the deck of the S.S. *Munargo*. A commotion from its interior prompted an opening which revealed a lively hawk's-bill turtle. The officers of the ship took the turtle to New York and found it a more congenial home at the aquarium where it continued to live in vast content under the appropriate name of Jonah.

The main purpose of a shark's teeth is not for chewing but for cutting up food. A goat might chew his dinner of tin cans, but a shark is not so particular, depending entirely upon its powerful digestive apparatus to take care of them.

Being a cannibal, there is nothing a shark likes better than a chunk of another shark. With such choice bait, and just for the sport of it, I hooked a fighting terror one day and after battling with him to the limit of my strength with a 200-foot rope I brought him alongside my diving-boat. Then, bending over from the deck with two men behind me, our united pull on the line lifted the shark's head out of the water and a native boy reached down with a sheath-knife to lance the hook loose to let the fish go.

As the knife did its work, the shark's powerful tail lashed out at us, striking my men who, in stumbling, pushed me overboard. For one hair-raising instant I

236

hung helpless in the air and the next thing I knew I was astride the back of the plunging devil, and was actually riding him under the sea! In the churned-up water I could not see which was the way to the surface, but striking out wildly I eventually reached it. Flat on deck my men, with necks stretched out like turtles, were fearfully and tearfully waiting for my return. Good fellows, but, after all, merely waiting. It was lucky for me that the teeth of the shark had not closed on some part of my anatomy or even my clothing, for I certainly had been close to my finish.

In spite of the evil propensities of sharks, they were essential to my undersea drama. Once I staged an expensive attraction, spending $250 on bait in an endeavour to get one shark to cavort through a vitally important scene. While the creatures had always been plentiful hitherto, this time no sharks were to be seen in our chosen location. Hundreds of pounds of tempting morsels were spread round the vicinity, but no sharks appeared. For a week we continued our endeavours, but had no luck. Mutterings and murmurings were growing in volume among my natives about the glorious time we had had with sharks when once we used a sleek black bull for bait. Like the legendary luck of the black cat, they were sure that a sleek black bull would bring the sharks. It was a whim, I knew, but to please them I sent out a call for a black bull.

While a plentiful supply of loggerhead turtles, sheep

and pigs had failed to tempt any sharks, I read in the papers that an epidemic of them had spread panic along the Atlantic beaches. The sharks were roving with a vengeance. And with this news came the response to our call for a bull. A man appeared ready to offer up a black-and-white cow.

I paid a personal visit to his proffered sacrifice and saw immediately that her days were numbered. She was literally dying on her feet. The wily owner had decided to cash in on the cow before the cow cashed in on him, but his price was prohibitive, so I decided to continue with the bait we had. Then we received word that the price of the cow had been greatly reduced, and I planned to acquire her the next time I visited the port for supplies.

Entering the harbour next day, we sighted a suspicious-looking object moving down the current. Yes, it was our high-priced cow! Fate had stepped in and delivered her into our hands. Weary of waiting, she had succumbed to her ailments, and her owner, to comply with the law, had taken the carcass out to sea. Under the heat of the tropical sun it was fast turning green.

Nevertheless, getting to the windward side of it, I ordered a rope to be thrown. Time was the essence of the enterprise and the speed and deftness of the roping would have done credit to a wild-west cowboy. Will Rogers himself couldn't have done a neater job. Then the crew began to grumble. They were positive

239

no shark would ever bite into that, but I ordered that the carcass be displayed to the sharks. Two hundred feet to the leeward we let it drift, then started to draw it toward our scene, but always we carefully stayed to windward. There was no other position livable under the circumstances.

Soon the most voracious-looking monster of a shark made its appearance. Swiftly it circled around the cow and an instant later it had dashed into the carcass and was tossing it up as a horse would shake a feed-bag of oats. We could hear its head thumping about in the interior of the unfortunate cow. Like the tom-toms of the jungle, the sound seemed to serve as a call, for almost immediately a lively school of sharks appeared and we shot our big undersea scene successfully.

A celebration was in order, for to add to the triumphant culmination of our fine day's work, it was Thanksgiving Day. Though in a foreign port, our chef had seen to it that we had a turkey. It was a fine-looking twenty-pounder and my hungry staff prepared to do it justice.

Dressed and refreshed we sat down to dinner, but no one had reckoned on the influence of the old green cow. It made cowards of us all. No sooner did anyone lift a succulent morsel to his mouth than he put it down again. We were hungry but without the courage to continue. Dinner came to an abrupt end. My disgruntled staff went off to town for a change of scenery and some liquid refreshment. About midnight they arrived *en masse* for a raid on the turkey. They felt equal to it by then. But a search of the icebox revealed that the bird had flown. Our chef, after the time-honoured custom of all coloured servants in the hospitable South, had carried it off to his waiting relatives. There wasn't a wishbone or even a pin-feather left. Needless to say, my staff was ready for breakfast early next morning.

Chapter XV

SUCKER-FISH

THE late Prince of Monaco told me a story about sucker-fish which in brief reveals the nature of these odd little citizens of the sea. As is well known, the prince had devoted his life and fortune to oceanography. He was out in the Mediterranean one day when an immense shark was captured which he decided to preserve for his collection. In order to hoist the monster on board his yacht, he had a heavy boom lowered over the side. The crew had hooked tackle to the shark and were about to haul it from the sea when the prince gave orders to capture the several sucker-fish, or remora, which were darting about the shark.

This was no easy task in the open sea but the men went to work. The remora simply refused to be caught. Despairing of ever being able to capture any of them, the prince told the men to abandon their efforts and haul up the shark.

With a chugging of winches and crunching of gears, the shark rose from the sea. It was halfway out of the water when with a whirl and a flash three or four sucker-fish shot alongside the body of the shark, and

"They hold on with bull-dog tenacity"
SUCKER FISH (REMORA) ON THE PECTORAL FINS OF A SHARK

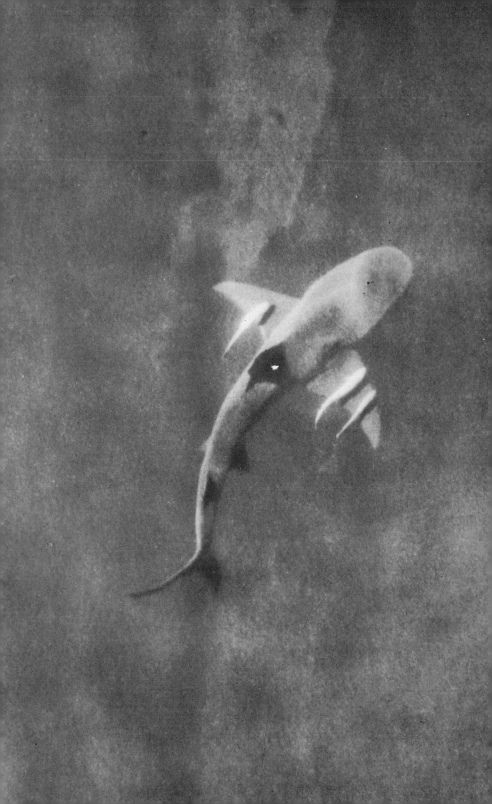

clapping their suction disks to his skin, hung on like grim death. The shark was lifted clear of the water. The boom swung over, and when the prince's big specimen was deposited safely on the deck the sucker-fish, wide-eyed and gasping, were still hanging on.

The adhesive powers of these fishes are truly remarkable. They hold on with bull-dog tenacity and at times will allow themselves to be torn asunder rather than release their grip. To the ancients this fish was known as Echeneis, or "The Ship Holder," for it was believed that they possessed the power to hold a vessel motionless. Pliny, the naturalist, wrote, "Why should our fleets and armadas at sea carry such turrets on the walls and forecastles, when one little fish is able to arrest and stay perforce, our goodly and tall ships?"

While we may scoff at such ideas, it is a fact that sucker-fish often get free rides by adhering to the bottom of vessels, sea-turtles, whales, or even humans. The adhesive apparatus with which Nature has endowed the sucker-fish is very simple. It consists of an area of corrugated skin on the top of the head which operates by creating a vacuum when pressed against any object. It works on the same principle as the concave rubber cups with hooks attached, used for hanging light pictures. The sucker-fish, however, has gone one better than man. While the ordinary suction disk can be attached only to a smooth, even surface, that of the remora will adhere firmly to rough, uneven surfaces like the horny file-like skin of a shark. To the naked eye, shark skin appears smooth or with a roughened, sandpaper-like surface, but under a magnifying glass it is seen to bristle with curved sharp-pointed claws. Scientists who are familiar with sharks can determine the species merely by an examination of a single square inch of skin. With a few exceptions, each kind of shark, though inclined to roam, has its own particular domain in the ocean, but anywhere and everywhere in tropical and sub-tropical seas seems to be home to the homeless sucker-fish. All sharks look alike to them. If no shark is about, any old thing that moves will do, turtle, fish, boat or floating timber. Their preference is for sharks, and in many places they are regarded as the pilot fish of sharks.

I have made repeated studies in an effort to prove or disprove the assertion that they actually guide the sharks to food and warn them of danger. From my observations I have come to the conclusion that, indirectly, a sucker-fish may transmit some warning or information to the shark. In this manner the remora may "pilot" the shark just as certain species of birds who perch on the backs of jungle beasts may warn their hosts of danger by flying about and uttering cries of alarm. I believe, however, that any such service is merely coincidental and involuntary, and that the sucker-fish is just a hanger-on, taking advantage of the speedier fish to carry him about and provide him with free meals, which consist mainly of scraps of food left over or missed by his gluttonous host. But at times I have seen sucker-fish that were apparently doing some voluntary and intelligent piloting. One day I planted a piece of bait among the reefs on the sea bottom, and as a shark manœuvred about searching for the titbit by sense of smell, its family of sucker-fish would let go, dart forward ten or twelve feet, nip at the bait and dash back again to the shark. This action was repeated again and again until the shark seemed to be guided to the bait which it gulped down without so much as a "thank you" to its pilots.

But I do not believe that the sucker-fish carry out such manœuvres for the benefit of the shark. There is method in their madness. Their motives are purely selfish. They have learned that when a shark dines he is untidy and observes no rules of etiquette. Shreds of food escape from his rapacious jaws. By being close at hand the remoras pick up an easy living. Do not believe for a moment that the sharks are grateful or even friendly with the sucker-fish. There is no love lost between the two. The shark hates everyone but himself, and the sucker-fish are careful to keep just out of reach of the monster's jaws. On more than one occasion I have seen the companionable sucker-fish actually dining on their living host, eating into an open wound in his flesh and gleefully enjoying the feast.

Circus riders are no more deft and nimble in their

movements than sucker-fish. When a shark glides close to the sea bottom, or moves among coral forests and reefs where he might come in contact with some jagged projection, the remoras release their grip, turn a somersault and instantly affix themselves to some other portion of the shark's anatomy. They can release themselves and take a new hold in a moment. They are also extremely swift in their motions when the shark circles about in search of food. They vary in size from a few inches to several feet in length. While museum specimens are rare and usually quite small I have captured sucker-fish almost as large as a baseball bat. This is a good comparison, as they resemble baseball bats in the shape and lines of their bodies.

On one occasion I captured a sucker-fish nearly three feet long and holding it by the tail, playfully swung it as if it had been a bat. Its head slapped against the side of the ship's cabin and instantly the adhesive disk stuck fast. I couldn't pull the fish away and even when I released my grip, it remained hanging there.

Clowning about in their undersea arena, these harlequins of the deep have both amused and annoyed me. From my deep-sea chamber I have seen sharks drowned in capture, and in their death struggle I have seen them roll over in the pale green light of the depths to reveal sucker-fish groping about on their expansive white chests, like infants clinging to their mothers' breasts. It was almost pathetic to watch them holding fast to a dead body as if it were their only hope and refuge. But the instant that the deceased man-eater was set upon and torn to pieces by his fellows, the sucker-fish would shift from the dead to the living. At times of such carnage dozens of sucker-fish could be seen cruising about, darting this way and that, searching for a likely spot on which to cling.

My photosphere offers a most inviting mooring-place for these homeless orphans. It is only natural that they frequently become attached to it. No doubt the metal walls of the chamber appear to them as some great sea monster whose size promises plenty of food in left-overs. The smooth surface offers easy sticking for the creatures, and it is quite possible that they enjoy admiring their own reflections in the glass window of the chamber.

I have made many photographic studies of these fishes before my window, and have had unique opportunities to study the underside working of their suction pads, and watch the corrugated ridges of the sucking grips as they quiver and cling to the outside of the glass.

I once saw a colony of a dozen or so performing apparently for my sole benefit, like so many trained pets. It was then that I discovered that a loaf of bread, weighted and lowered into the sea was choice food for them. They went for it like children after sweets, their big frog-mouths and fine sharp teeth making quick work of the welcome meal. After that I gave them each day their favourite loaf of bread. Shortly after I was forced to part company with them. I was preparing to film a very important scene, and it was essential that I had a perfectly clear field of vision so that my lenses could penetrate to the limit of their reach. A scene costing a small fortune was about to be shot when suddenly the school of sucker-fish interrupted my work. Despite every attempt to drive them away they would persist in coming across my field of vision or fastening themselves to the glass. Then, to make matters worse, the entire lot of remoras came swarming about my window and to my amazement I discovered that they were depositing a jelly-like mucus on the glass. Immediately I summoned a diver to descend and clean it, but there was every likelihood that the sucker-fish would return and spoil the scene. So I planned a little farewell party for them. Into the sea my men lowered a big loaf of bread containing a surprise. It was dynamite. Down into the sea came the loaded loaf and the sucker-fish rushed at it like hungry wolves. Slowly my assistants moved the farewell banquet away from the boat and my photochamber. When at a safe distance, they fired the charge. There were no more remoras.

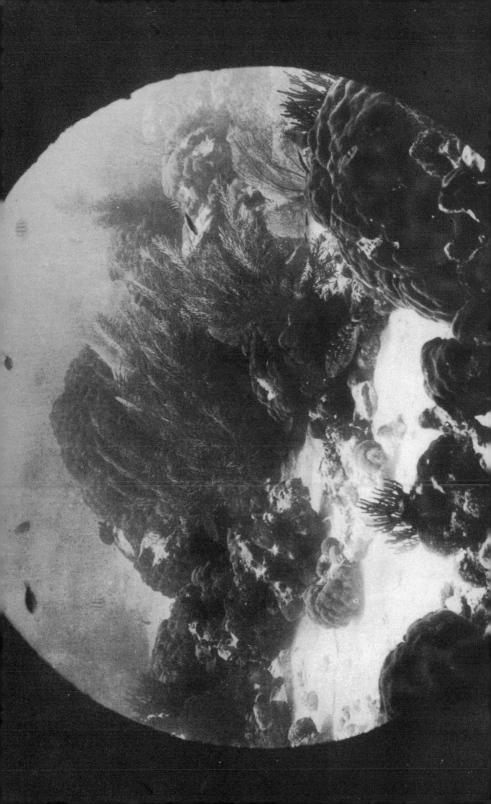

Chapter XVI

EXPLORING THE CORAL JUNGLES

TO descend into the mysterious and extravagantly beautiful region of ocean depths for the Field Museum of Natural History was to be my next experience.

From the time I had taken my first picture of a fish "at home" beneath the waters of Chesapeake Bay, scientists had evinced a lively interest in my photosphere and its possibilities. Here was something new and challenging. With telescopes the heavens had been swept in the search for the secrets of the stars. Now the Williamson Tube with its submarine eye provided a means of solving the riddles of the ocean.

Many celebrated zoologists and oceanographers had descended in my submarine chamber and had pried into the private lives of fishes. I had made many photographs for purely scientific purposes, and had been associated with the work of two major scientific expeditions. My first introduction to field work under the sea was with Dr. George Engelhardt of the Brooklyn Museum while engaged in obtaining specimens for a coral reef group. Later I joined forces with Dr. Roy W.

251

"Into the mysterious region of the ocean's depths . . ."
DEEP SEA FERNS AND BRAIN CORAL MAKE EXQUISITE DESIGNS

Miner of the American Museum of Natural History in obtaining forty tons of coral and invaluable under-ocean records from the great barrier reef at Andros Island for the museum.

With the peculiar knowledge gained through years of explorations I was by no means a novice at scientific work in the deep when the Field Museum requested me to obtain for them undersea settings for their proposed display of West Indian fish life at home in the sea. I gladly consented. I was to lead my first scientific expedition.

"Material for seven habitat groups of Bahama fishes, with coral and accessories," was the museum's description of its requirements. That description, expressed so concisely, covered a vast amount of detail.

Suppose, for instance, I had been required to collect material for a habitat group of West Indian natives. First, I would have to depict a family at home, man, woman and child, their palm-thatched hut surrounded by trees and shrubbery. The donkey, chickens, dogs and cats, mocking birds, lizards, even the insects in the vicinity would have to be recorded along with the litter in the yard, husks of coco-nuts, banana peel, mango seeds, and rubbish. I would have to make photographic studies and colour sketches of all this, with the natives engaged in their customary tasks. Perhaps the man would be smoking with the ashes from his pipe dropped beside him, and just to show how important little things are, those ashes as they appeared on the ground where they fell would have to be recorded in colour and detail, just as faithfully as the face of the man who had made them.

It would be the same with a habitat group of fish. Even the ripples on the sandy ocean floor would have to be recorded, for they are just as important as the face of a man-eating shark which might be the central figure in the setting.

Obtaining the seven habitat groups of Bahaman fishes meant far more than a fishing-jaunt. I was to conduct a completely equipped expedition to the West Indies, and there under clear, tropical waters, obtain studies of the inhabitants of the deep, from man-eating sharks to butterfly-fish. I was to visit the fishes in their home in the coral fairyland, record their life movements and habits, their colour changes; how they appear to make love, fight, make up, and consume one another.

The desired species were to be lifted out of the sea together with their massive coral homes, surrounding friends and enemies dead and alive, and shipped to the Field Museum. But not until the photographic and other records were completed could I begin the actual work of collecting the specimens for the groups, work that would involve, in addition to the necessary skill and scientific knowledge a prodigious amount of hard manual labour. But it was labour in which I took keen delight, for later a visitor to the Field Museum could

253

step into the Hall of the Ocean Floor and look with wonder at these sections of life faithfully recreated with all the glory and fascination of their watery world. If the public couldn't go to the mountain, we would bring the mountain to them, so to speak. We would accomplish this tremendous assignment of bringing the bottom of the sea to Chicago, and have a good time doing it, all within a museum budget.

In one respect I was fortunate. I didn't have to hunt for my working locations, for I had already seen them near a little palm-studded island called Sandy Cay, in the Bahama Islands. There on my honeymoon the previous year I had cruised near to the exact coral forest I now desired to invade. There I could lift my great coral specimens and complete my undersea records with the capture of myriads of beautiful rainbow-hued fishes, along with others which were ugly and repulsive.

It was a blustery day early in March when I left Chicago. In its light mantle of snow, the Field Museum beside Lake Michigan afforded a striking contrast to the waving palm-trees on the sunny isles that awaited me in the tropics. To add to the pleasure and problems of the moment, an important item of our equipment and baggage was a tiny bundle of humanity, my six-weeks'-old daughter, Sylvia, a new member of the Williamson Submarine Expedition, born in Chicago at the same time that the idea of the expedition was born, and now

HE "JULES VERNE," MOTHER-BOAT OF THE WILLIAMSON TUBE

quite naturally going with her parents on their work of exploration—to the bottom of the sea.

Creeping through the fog-bound shipping of New York harbour we steamed out to the broad Atlantic on March 18th, and in three days entered the port of Nassau where, after years of continued undersea exploration, my vessels, crew and equipment were established. But weeks of preparation would be necessary to this particular undertaking. Our museum work must proceed along its own particular lines. The haste and extravagant expenditure sometimes necessary to film production were not called for.

Near the water's edge our laboratory provided roomy living- and working-quarters, with store-rooms for gear, dark-rooms, and other necessities. And in the harbour our odd-looking craft were anchored near the trim flagship *Standard J.* The outstanding vessel in freak design was the *Jules Verne*, mother boat of the Williamson Tube and my undersea photographic studio and equipment. Next in original design were two pontoons fastened together with shearlegs and overhead beams bearing chain hoists and gear which I intended to use for lifting huge coral formations from the bed of the sea. This odd little fleet which would include numerous motor-boats and tenders and our newly chartered smack with wells for keeping fish alive, would play a large part in bringing about the museum results.

On the shores of several of the outer islands I planned

"Full diving suits and equipment were needed"
DIVERS AT WORK IN ROCK CORAL

to set up beach camps at locations nearest to the big corals and other specimens I intended to gather from the sea-floor. Such camps called for tents, cots, furnishings and supplies, including mountains of tinned food, rolls of mosquito netting, to say nothing of a fresh-water supply, perhaps the most important requirement of all. And as hundreds of fish of all kinds and sizes were to be captured, there were all manner of fish-nets, traps, grains and harpoons, lines and hooks; the latter varying in size from immense shark hooks larger than umbrella handles to tiny pin hooks for the little fellows.

The coral-lifting process was more than a weighty one. Often these corals are veritable trees—the bigger the better for museum purposes—weighing several tons, and as firmly rooted to the bed of the sea as forest trees on land. In fact, they are even more securely rooted, for the roots of corals are of hard limestone calling for crowbars, sledges, drills and possibly dynamite in order to free them.

While native divers without suits or helmets would serve for collecting the smaller specimens, full diving-suits and equipment were needed where long periods of work beneath the sea were necessary.

Besides these there were tongs, grabs, grappling-irons and similar devices for lifting coral masses, while last, but by no means least, were the cameras, plates and film, sketch pads, note-books, canvas, paints and

259

colours, for we were to photograph or sketch our
specimens in their natural surroundings before lifting
them to the world above.

On April 14th everything needful had been secured,
and under ideal weather conditions I moved out to sea
with my little fleet and headed for my chosen location
which was about eight miles from Nassau, between
Sandy Cay and Little Green Cay, with Rose Island
stretching across the horizon to the south.

Immediately there was a hum of activity aboard the
Jules Verne. The big studio windows received their
final polish and the observation and photographic
chamber was lowered into the sea through the well or
opening in the vessel's hull. Section after section of the
tube was attached and the flexible submarine tube
neared the bottom. Climbing down the tube, I adjusted
the ear 'phones, glanced about at my undersea surroundings and signalled to the men to lower away
until the chamber of the photosphere was within a
few inches of the floor of the sea. Then, responding to
my submarine directions, the *Jules Verne* moved ahead.
Before I left the surface of the sea I knew from indications that we were near a maze of reefs. "A labyrinth
of coral" describes the nature of the coral forest several
square miles in area which I wished to enter and explore.

Skimming over the bed of the ocean, which was
swept by the current until the white sand bottom
showed ripples like a windswept desert, I saw the coral

kingdom looming in the distance. Majestically, like a true forest on the edge of a plain, arose great coral masses, dimly outlined against the translucent background of the horizon of this wonder world under the sea. Slowly we closed in until we were in the midst of a sea garden at the very portals of the forest.

Now I knew that our group material was near, if not directly at hand. All about me the corals teemed with life. The scene was brilliantly illuminated by the light of the sun, for down to sixty feet, under ideal conditions, I can observe and photograph without the aid of my banks of artificial lights.

In this paradise, as though painted on a backcloth, I could see fish of the most exotic hues lurking in the coral. A boar grunt stared idly at a pair of butterfly-fishes escorting their tiny offspring right past his nose, and on into a miniature forest of lavender sea feathers. Sleek, brilliant slippery dicks, pudding wives, and old wives, mingled with sailors' choice; and down in a grotto, a wobbly cow-fish came poking her horns through the parade. In shadowy nooks were parrot-fish as brilliantly coloured as their feathered namesakes, along with angelfish, gold, black, and green—tropical beauties, only to be surpassed by a gorgeous queen triggerfish which glided serenely past, her dainty fins like trailing draperies of blue, green and gold.

Signalling a direction to the mother ship above, I moved close to a coral head where yellow grunts were massed by the hundreds, motionless against purple sea fans, rising from the giant clump of Orbicella. Here I stopped and watched the silent drama of the undersea.

A more peaceful school of fish could hardly be imagined. They seemed to sleep, yet their eyes, like perfect gems, flashed light. A closer view revealed them all wide-awake, vibrating with life, their motionless grouping a clever camouflage. The risk of being devoured is much greater to each individual if moving about in the open. Lazily the column disbanded, but with a few graceful turns the mass re-formed with all heads and eyes turned one way. Then suddenly there was a flurry and two of the grunts paired off and faced each other with fins extended and mouths wide open. They approached head on and then, "Smack!" it looked like a kiss! Then quivering with animation they sidled off together, lips pressed tight, disappearing through holes in the coral and on into the shadows.

I felt as though I was spying on petting parties in the park and shifted my gaze from the grunts to a pair of schoolmasters. There it was again—the gaping mouths pressed close, then they broke apart to disport in a flashing chase, then contact again and again, with sometimes a third party pursuing and biting the back of one of the pair engaged. Could this be the eternal triangle?

Then all this inexplicable business ceased in an instant.

Some signal of alarm must have gone out, for all the fish dashed quickly to shelter. Alert, they watched from cover, eyes rolling up and around. The next moment the sea was darkened, as thousands of big hungry jacks invaded the submarine Eden. Silently they flashed past and were gone. Scarcely had the raiders vanished when the bright-hued reef fish came forth and resumed life as before, with the tropical sun pouring a barrage of light rays down through the ever-changing waves at the surface, causing a weaving pattern of light to flow over them and all forms of life below.

What an amazing group for the museum! I marked this as number one—for consideration. I had not yet entered the reefs proper and could afford to look round. Was not the Field Museum's code "Excellence in all things"? But a feeling of relaxation and languour stole over me. My eyes feasted on the wonders of the sea as I sat at ease. The strain of the city and civilization melted away. I was spell-bound—lost in restful reverie as the spiritual influence of the undersea held me, and time passed by as nothing. I was strangely content.

But this mental drifting with the tide could not endure for long. My instinct to photograph spurred me to action, and I shot movies and still pictures at a tremendous rate. Working my camera with both hands busy, I caught a signal from far above through my ear 'phones, and suddenly realized that I had momentarily

forgotten my wife and her wish to give baby Sylvia a first glimpse—a fish-eye view of life in the deep.

I scrambled to the surface to meet the little one and her mother. The wee "Captain" was all dressed up for the occasion, wearing her full naval uniform and cap. But how were we to get her down the tube? Later, her many trips below were made in a knapsack on my back, but her début into the society of the undersea world resolved itself into a relay method of transportation. My faithful native diving boys and crew were gathered about, all grinning in admiration at the smiling water baby about to be rocked in the cradle of the deep. Grasping the plan of action and following my lead the men poured down the tube after me, stationing themselves at regular intervals up the tube to the top. In this manner each man in turn could reach up, take hold of the "Captain" and pass her between his legs to the man below. With this hand-me-down method she was lowered as quietly and gently as a descending star, from her mother's embrace on deck to my arms below. Although her eyes were wide with wonder, she made no outcry. She liked it!

Up went the boys to their stations on deck and soon my wife came tripping down—no lowering or hoisting her as we sometimes did with visitors. She had had her muscles well trained to climbing the flexible tube.

Perhaps my feelings were like those of an airman when he first takes his offspring for a jaunt in the

"The wee 'Captain' was all dressed up for the occasion"
THE WILLIAMSON FAMILY INSIDE THE "JULES VERNES"

clouds. I knew there was no real danger, yet at first I could not suppress a slight feeling of apprehension for the little "Captain's" safety. But as I placed her on her mother's knee, she entirely reassured us both by her smile and an eager lurch to the big studio window where she took her first wondrous look into the strange world of the fishes, trying her best to thrust her chubby fists through the glass and seize the bright-coloured creatures of the deep.

That night with all at rest, and the *Jules Verne* anchored securely in the open sea, I cruised over the top of the coral forest. The sea was dead calm, and in the bright moonlight I experienced a weird sensation by leaning directly over the bow of the speeding motor-boat as it skimmed over the surface of the sea. It was like flying, for the amazing transparency of the water revealed the moonlit sea bottom, six, ten and even more fathoms below, with the ghost-like coral formations reaching up toward the surface. Changing the direction of the boat at will, I followed the winding passages outlined by the clear white sea bottom, the exposed reef platform in and around the great rising masses of coral jungle.

Geologically, the Bahama Islands are described as hardened ridges of marl or sea bottom thrust up from below. Great ocean depths surround and tongue into the island group, and the hundreds of islands and small cays rest mainly on a great plateau. At one time this

"She took her first look into the strange world of fishes"
CONVICT FISH, SERGEANT MAJORS, AND SCHOOLMASTERS

plateau supporting the islands was one hundred feet higher than it is now. Apparently a great drop took place, and while there are no signs of volcanic or other force to make these changes, the islands are said to be steadily on the rise again.

The coral forest over which I was now speeding in the moonlight might, in a few thousand years, grow up to form an island, a true coral island. However, the rocky formation of the Bahamas indicates that the mass of coral formed through time in this region has been ground up by the sea and mixed with the shells and dust of minute sea organisms, so that these islands, formed of Æolian rock, are only partly of coral formation.

But now the virgin coral forest below bloomed serenely in its element. Schools of fish scurried through the dark grottoes of this strange world I had come to explore.

The next day I hurried off to Nassau to meet the final, and in some respects the most important, member of the expedition, Mr. Leon L. Pray, taxidermist extraordinary to the Field Museum. I have had the pleasure of initiating many interesting people into the undersea realm, but this was my first guest who was a master taxidermist. His work was to be an important feature of the group reproduction. It is not generally known that museums seldom use the actual body or skins of fish for exhibition. The most enduring are obtained by making a cast of the fish in life, and from this cast, which records every scale and marking, make a model. The work of colouring and finishing the model is later carried out in full detail, and the fish made to appear as it did in life. In this particular work Mr. Pray was an expert.

By noon the next day with my undersea equipment in full operation, I had not only entered the coral jungle, but, by cruising around in the reef area and exploring from my position in the observation chamber at the sea floor, I had found the very centre of the coral mass, where I was delighted to find a large, open space affording a safe anchorage for my fleet.

From this anchorage, with Pray at my side rapidly compiling notes and pictorial records with me, I piloted the photosphere back into the forest again. The sights along the coral avenues were amazing. All manner of fish-life nestled closely to the reefs. Suddenly the perfect peace and quiet was broken by a flurry in the white sand before us. We had disturbed some giant rays as we came upon them almost covered in the sea-bed. Frantically, like great black bats, they whipped their wing-like fins into action, and throwing the sand from their backs scurried away to settle again in some secluded spot. That is, if they were lucky, for, as if from nowhere, sharks suddenly appeared and pursued them. Down one lane we caught a glimpse of a big ray being taken by sharks and torn to pieces in their savage jaws. Not a shred was left except the tail.

The shark knows better than to eat this poisonous appendage. It is like a bull whip with a sharp poisoned lance in the end. Buried in the sand except for their periscopic eyes, the bat-like rays await their victims, their tails ever ready to flash in an upward curve like great steel springs carrying poison and death; but the shark's armoured hide, except for a small area, is too tough for the tail-battling rays.

Continuing on through the labyrinth of coral we turned a corner and suddenly found ourselves in a clustered region of stone trees. Almost breathless with wonder we drifted slowly the full length of the glade, recording the beauties that passed in panorama before us. At the end we found that our passage to the open sea beyond was blocked by a giant palmate, a golden tree beneath whose spreading branches we came to a stop. Rising majestically from the bulbous trunk of the tree like hundreds of outstretched arms with upturned hands, the majority of the branches reached valiantly toward the life-giving ocean current.

Pray had been working like mad with brush, paint and pencils. About one grunt an hour was the only sound that came from him. The colours outside the photosphere window were soon reproduced in his sketches, which fell one by one to the floor. Apart from the click and hum of my cameras, silence reigned within the chamber.

This golden branching palmate before us, like the

others in the glade, was a growing tree—yet as dead as a tombstone. A monument of pure limestone. The only living thing about it is its coating of animal life which is made up of millions of tiny polyps that swarm over it as they build it. Imagine the ambition of a colony of polyps, starting from nothing and building such a fantastic structure.

What manner of creature is this prolific polyp whose artistic energy is supreme? Scientists who have explored his world through the all-seeing eye of the microscope know all his family secrets, have watched his offspring and counted the ribs of his calyx.

Perhaps it will suffice to say that the polyp is a queer little jelly-fish with a body as transparent as glass, and though he may be no larger than the proverbial pin-head, his body is supported by a complicated skeleton which he leaves to posterity when he dies.

When searching for food in the sea-water about him, the polyp can throw out as lively a set of tentacles as his big brother, the octopus. Going one better than the octopus, his tentacles are loaded with poisonous darts to shoot down his victims if out of reach. The polyp is a glutton. If he ever has a stomach-ache he must hurt all over, for his stomach is practically all of him. He fills up with food that is often alive and kicking. These inside guests are permitted to visit each other and multiply until he decides to take them into his final mouth for digestion.

271

It was in connection with this that the scientists discovered his means of colouring his building enterprises. Transporting a section of living coral to the laboratory table, they discovered through their lenses that polyps are particular about their menu. One group has a craving to feed on microscopic organisms that look and are coloured like oranges, while another group feed on minute creatures of a different colour, and therein lies the answer. If an army of polyps were labouring on empty stomachs the coral creation would be as pale as their skeletons, pure limestone white. But lo and behold, when the orange-eating colony all fill up with their "citrus" diet, as is likely in the case of the palmate coral, the yellow contents show through their bulging transparent stomachs and the tree appears golden. That's one way the colours are spread artistically over the coral mountains.

So much for the polyp who chooses to build his monument of stone, but what must we think when we see the amazing results of one who builds a structure that is flexible? This polyp lays down a foundation of a horny substance to support his intricate masterpiece. The result is the gorgonias, the name the scientists have given these grotesque and bending varieties, a family which can boast of sea-plumes, exquisite lace-like sea-fans, sea-whips, sea-rods and weird bush forms, all looking like plant life but actually living animal organisms. A few feet farther on the corallines appear, looking like gorgonias and animal life, but being just as much plant life as the grass that grows in the sea bed.

It is a complex trail, this trek of creation. Does Nature in the sea below imitate Nature above it, or is it the reverse? In the depths grow trees in gardens surrounded by shrubs, bushes and flowers, and gay-coloured fish take the place of birds.

All life, it is said, came from the sea. Maybe the parrot-fish of the submarine jungle is a distant ancestor of the parrot that asks for a nut. We could go on for ever with comparisons, but hesitate we must, when we ponder and question what salt-water ancestors adorn humanity's family tree. Are polyp-like propensities included in the make-up of us humans who are, as a matter of fact, nearly all water—and salt water at that? Just where on the journey did we shed our fins and lose our gills and leave the fish behind?

But here we were at the bottom of the sea to work and not to ask questions. Pray grunted again indicating the passing of time. Around me the photosphere was littered with the results of our recording expedition, yet there was more and more to be seen. Drawing nearer to the giant palmate we were both attracted to a mixture of colours smeared around the bulbous trunk of the gold-sheathed creation. Clearly defined was a patch of olive green. The work of racketeer polyps. They had invaded this structure built up by the hard work of others, muscled in, and made themselves at home. The result was a blotch of contrasting colour, interesting to study along with the invaders who most likely were partial to a diet of some minute sea-life the colour of olives, and were green because of a stomach full of them.

Soon we perceived that these patches were common. They were everywhere about us, adding greatly to the troubles of tropical fish who tried to change their colours to match their surroundings as they swam inquisitively by. It looked to us as though Nature had gone quite mad, yet all was toned into perfect harmony in this watery world of wonders.

I wondered if any artist could faithfully capture the whole sweep and key to such a riot of colours, such kaleidoscopic effects, all shifting in the changing lights?

Suddenly it was as though some unseen hand were ringing down the curtain on the gorgeous undersea setting. An ominous drab cloud was blotting out the picture. I glanced upward. Above my chamber the transparent water no longer glowed with the ambient pale green light, shot through with effulgent sunshine. It was getting dark. The next instant I had forgotten corals, beauty, colour, everything below, and was scurrying up the flexible tube with the records we had made.

Gaining the deck of the *Jules Verne* I saw that lowering black storm-clouds darkened the sky and hung like a pall over the sea and the islands. The atmosphere was heavy and oppressive. The sea was like black oil with the breaking surf on the cays and reefs looming in patches of white through the semi-darkness. An hour or so earlier the sea had appeared a smiling, glorious expanse of liquid sapphire. But now it was ugly and threatening, with sinister power, to lash itself into fury. And the reefs below! With their outjutting masses, they were like crouching monsters, stretching sharp talons upward, ready to grasp us and drag us down to destruction.

Working quickly we raised the tube and photosphere until it was completely housed within the *Jules Verne*, and found our way out of the coral pocket and into the anchorage in the centre of the menacing reefs. Here we must stay, for before we could find a safe passage out of the labyrinth the gale would be upon us. We were trapped.

The fleet must ride out the storm in the centre of the reef area. I shouted orders rapidly as the men worked like demons to get out all possible moorings. Our heaviest anchors were dropped, our heaviest hawsers made fast, and everything movable on deck and inside was lashed down.

This turn in events called for a quick shift in my plan of action. If we could not work in the sea we could work ashore. Our priceless records were quickly collected and wrapped in some waterproof material. Some of the crew rapidly stripped the Rose Island camp of Mr. Pray's belongings. There he had prepared to do some of his taxidermy. We didn't finish a minute too soon. Just as the last boatload was transferred to the flagship in the open sea, the inky-black clouds which had been hanging like a canopy over our heads, opened up and spilled out an ocean of rain.

Instantly our vessels, the nearby islands, everything, was blotted out. But there was one consolation. My fleet was safely moored with a good crew aboard, and as I headed with my working staff to our comfortable laboratory at Nassau, I knew that we were not in for a hurricane. Of that I felt certain. I had been through too many of them not to know the symptoms. What we were in for, judging from the direction and indication of the storm, was a period of winds and wetness that would last for at least a week.

Chapter XVII

WET WINDS

A S expected, with each dawn came more rain. However, we had plenty to do. There was the pile of unanswered mail and small things that became important, such as getting a haircut.

Setting the main stage for action to combat the wet spell, taxidermy instead of film business now prevailed in the Nassau laboratory. Moulding plaster by the ton had been moved in. Selected native help stood by with mouths agape in amazement while Pray opened up his coffin-like boxes, laying out a profusion of cutlery—long sharp scalpels, knives of all shapes and sizes, pincers and scissors of various designs, an endless assortment of glittering surgical instruments. Resting on the operating-table were tropical beauties of fish-life waiting to be offered up as a sacrifice to science. Meantime, Pray's assistant was sponging the specimens with a solution of alum.

Before the arrival of our taxidermist in Nassau I had arranged to keep him steadily supplied with all the fish specimens he could wish for from the tiniest reef butterfly-fish to huge sharks thirteen feet long. Now

277

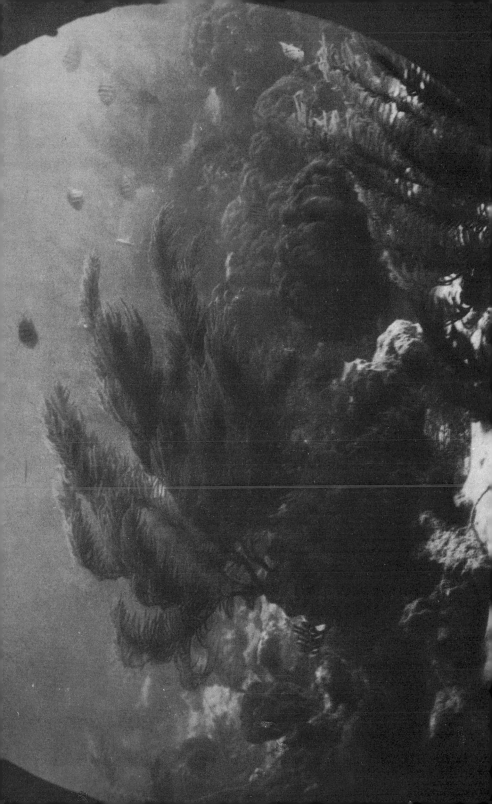

during the rainy spell, this scientific fishing could go on smoothly. Fresh live specimens just up from the deep were needed for the seven fish groups now clearly defined after our unique undersea observations.

As a scientific artist Pray took great pleasure in compiling his field notes and colour charts, but so glowing and vivid were some of the fish brought in they almost defied reproduction. But Pray would fondle them, cast them in true-to-life moulds and, missing no details, finally lay them down. Now a new discovery was made —Pray's art in cooking. His talents were unlimited, it seemed. With his keen scalpel he would lance open the back of each scientifically-recorded fish and produce a fillet, a morsel that was never to be washed or touched by human hands, not even his own. This was his system, and moreover, his method of cooking the fish was to tie the fillets in a linen bag and boil them like a pudding. The kind of fish involved meant nothing to him. Be it gorgeous or sinister to look upon, a fillet was just a fillet. Whether soap-fish, goat-fish, or angel-fish, they all went into the bag. However, the results were usually delicious.

Sitting down to dinner each night, with the rain beating a tattoo on the roof and dripping from the eaves, we would ask, "And what sort of fish is this, Pray tell." And Pray, like an oracle, would ponder awhile over the fillet in question and tell. To us they

THE OCEAN CURRENT
BENDS THE BRANCHES OF THE UNDERSEA CORAL TREES

all looked alike, though my keen olfactory sense warned me to be cautious.

Gradually we learned that Pray was a dietetic expert, well versed in his vitamins and calories. As doctors discuss their beautiful operations at the dinner-table, so Pray would enlarge on the effects of food on the human system.

Accustomed to getting at the inside of matters in his art of taxidermy, he acknowledged no privacy in his discussion of all things, from the universe to the atom. The study of foodstuffs was his hobby, and through various channels and ramifications he would usually conclude with the benefits to be derived from what he termed "roughage" to top off a meal. Backing up his statement, he would finish a hearty repast by slowly and systematically consuming a generous slab of raw cabbage. That there were benefits in this, he was positive.

With sleep or without it, Pray worked like a Trojan. The two hundredth cast was eventually completed. Pray's business was prospering, and we turned our minds to what he required for his great shark group. Five huge man-eaters were to appear in their lair in the coral reefs, and the entire group was to measure some forty-five feet across. The sharks must appear as in life, and to cast them in their various positions for the group, their bodies must be moulded while still fresh and pliable. This master group alone was a big order, requiring both strength and skill, not only in the work of casting the bulky man-eaters but in the capturing of the specimens and bringing them in alive.

Each morning, wet and windy, and without visible sunrise, meant the start of a long day in the open wave-tossed sea. In a stout motor-boat with my black crew beside me I would head for the turbulent reef area, searching through rain and spray to see if the fleet was still riding safely. The stormy routine included a round of inspection and the leaving of food and water supplies for the fleet. It was the same with each of the three beach camps, with the added thrills of landing supplies of lumber and materials on the shores of the islands through the surf. Taking time by the forelock, I was preparing to build the huge packing-cases that would house the big coral specimens for their long trip to Chicago. I thought out the size of the boxes to be made, and planned ways to pack the contents securely, providing a bed of comfort for our precious corals in these boxes that would be as large as an ordinary bedroom and made of the heaviest planking and timbers.

After each day in the open our return trips through the cuts and channels were always exciting, for we never failed to bring home some fighting demons, sharks or other large specimens.

One evening in the bay at Rose Island, we harpooned a huge ray which gave us a royal battle. The landing of this bat-like creature resulted in a curious experience. Suddenly the long line slackened, and peering over the side of the boat through the crystal clear water, we could see the ray circling about frantically, trying to hide in a hole beneath a coral ledge too small to receive it.

"It's looking for a place to die," muttered one of the natives.

There is something human about the face of a ray, and when we got it on deck this one seemed to be trying to say something—trying to utter some articulate words. With frightened eyes, its expression was almost pathetic. Three hours later I felt somewhat conscience-stricken when I realized that slowly, through the period of an hour or so, while seemingly lifeless, the ray had given birth to three perfect young ones. At first they were strange-looking objects, each tightly rolled up like a napkin in a ring, but presently they unfolded and revealed themselves as perfectly formed miniatures of their mother.

It was dark when we arrived at the laboratory and by the light of a lantern I showed the catch to Pray who planned to make casts of the whole ray family the first thing in the morning.

Then came the dawn of another blustery day and by seven o'clock I was ready with my crew to put out to sea. Pray had already finished the work of casting the rays, and just as I was leaving I saw him dangling his scalpel over the back of the mother ray with the zest of a surgeon about to perform an operation.

"Surely you're not going to eat that thing?" I asked as I made my exit, with a glance back at Pray who peered over his glasses, grinning like a Cheshire cat.

That day the going was rough. The rain stopped, but still threatened as the wind increased. From time to time the hot sun broke through and a steaming heat hung over us like a blanket that couldn't be thrown off, and, to make matters worse, while landing in the surf I had broken my only thermos bottle. Though parched with thirst, I still couldn't bring myself to drink from the metal container the native boys were using. As the day advanced it became hotter and hotter, until we seemed to bake. The black boys actually looked green at times. But the camp work continued and the piles of timber were hauled through the surf and stored above the high-tide line. Among the supplies were boatloads of sponge clippings, padding for the fragile corals; to keep them from blowing away, they were stored in our working tents. The sponge seemed quite harmless, but the handling of it spread an itch, adding new stings to our skins already tattooed with the marks of sandflies and mosquito bites.

To keep the boys working I had to use strategy; my bag of tricks was almost empty when I found I held magic in my trusty portable ciné-camera, which was usually strapped to my wrist. As long as the hum of the mechanism was heard by the men they were satisfied, even anxious to go on. They were not mere working men. They were all movie actors. I did film a good part of the action, but sometimes, I confess, the camera went on without a film in it.

This particular day I was actually filming some important scenes, when the camera stopped clicking. The men slowed down stupidly, slapping at their legs and bodies, for now they had time to think of the torturing bites of the insects, and other distractions.

That camera would have to be fixed; the film must have buckled, I thought, and if so would take but a few seconds to adjust, but I must have a dark-room to work in. Unfortunately there was no dark-room on the desolate, deserted island whose only regular inhabitants, at this time of the year, were wild pigs and land-crabs. Looking about the camp, I spied one of Pray's long grey packing-boxes that had once held his taxidermy gadgets. The box had been carefully made at the Field Museum and was almost airtight when its hinged top was shut down. There was my dark-room made to order. I didn't relish the idea of getting inside such a coffin-like hot-box, but there was no other way out *but* to go in.

To make sure there would be no light when I opened up the camera exposing the film, I called for a heavy tarpaulin to be used as an extra covering. I huddled inside, with the camera close under my face and chest, and was squeezed down as the lid was closed and the hasp snapped shut. In this position I could scarcely move a muscle except for the manipulation of my hands.

Outside my crew of black giants were scampering about like mad, not only throwing the heavy tarpaulin over my dark-room, but tucking it all about the box in the sand. Then to make sure that no wandering sunbeam should join me, they sat down on top of the box!

I opened the camera and my fingers soon told me that the film had not buckled. What was the trouble? The temperature inside of the box was even worse than I had expected. Sweat ran off me in streams, filling my eyes. I fumbled with the camera, shook it, and fiddled with every movable part. It was the shutter that was stuck. A grain of sand might be holding it. A few minutes more and I felt sure I could fix it, yet I seemed to be carrying the whole weight of the huddle of bodies above me as I worked on in the dark. What were those black devils yelling about? I tried to catch the meaning of their jumble of words. Now they were laughing in fiendish glee. A queer idea flashed through my mind. What if they did not respond to my signal for release? This could happen. Hadn't I damned them to Hades a hundred times, driven them like a slave driver, and, in emergencies, treated them like dogs, though I loved them all for the children they were by nature! Suppose, by some queer twist in their make-up, they turned on me now. Quite innocently they could sit there for a few minutes longer which might mean for me, good-bye. But the camera was humming. The shutter was clear. I was through, and I rapped out my signal for release.

"Comin' out, Boss," came the muffled reply. Throwing open the lid they helped me out, and we went on as before.

At the close of that long hot day I got home weary, but elated at the capture of a big bull shark to complete our group of man-eaters. Thirst had been forgotten, but now it returned with a vengeance along with a ravenous appetite—the reward of labour. By nine o'clock, after a shower and a change, and the bracing effects of a stiff whisky and soda, I was ready for dinner and quite happy. Taking a peep at the wee "Captain" who had heeded the sandman and was now sound asleep, I sat down with my wife and Pray, our usual family group. Without giving much thought to what I ate, I was laughingly relating the happenings of the day, when slowly my keen sense of smell began its nefarious work.

"What kind of fish am I eating?" I requested of Pray, while dark suspicion hung like a cloud over the sunshine of the moment.

"Why—that's ray," said Pray, looking as blandly innocent and smiling as he had that morning when I left him, scalpel in hand.

Dinner was over, for me.

The wet winds at last grew weary and quit. The sun shone brilliantly and a dead calm hung over land and sea.

During the period I had been compelled to abandon my underwater work, I had been making plans for the lifting of the huge coral trees from their home on the ocean's floor. In some cases the task would not be so very difficult, but it would certainly take something more than persuasion to dislodge that big golden palmate which blocked the roadway in the undersea glade.

My two best diving boys, Ward and Cinderella, were preening themselves with pride at being selected to help with the work down in the spooky shadows of the coral forest. Ward was the diver who almost won a full dress-suit from me once for fighting a shark, and Cinderella had had a long string of hair-raising adventures with me.

After a few hours' work the *Jules Verne* was again floating over the top of the forest. From the photosphere below I guided the equipment through the dangerous passages until we reached the end of the glade and again stopped by the huge yellow palmate with its bulbous trunk and mottled patches of colour.

I marvelled at the tranquillity below. The storm we had experienced above meant nothing in these untouched depths. To sit motionless and succumb to its peculiar fascination would have been perfect bliss, but

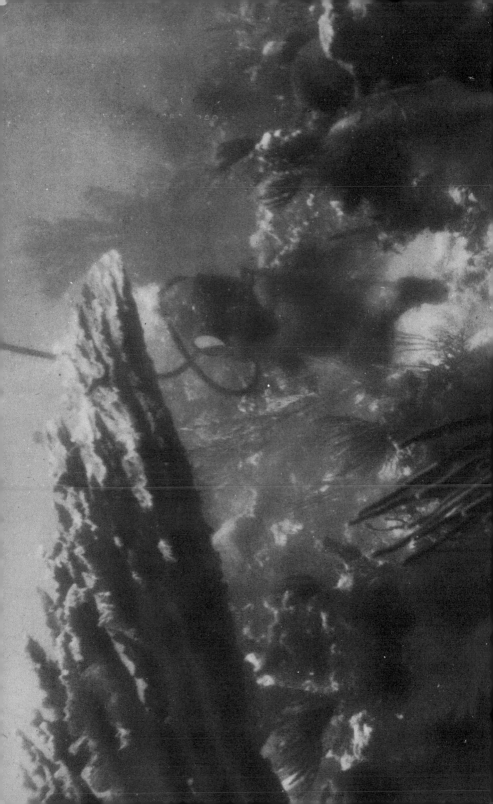

instead I began at once to consider how this coral tree, which I had set my heart upon, might be lifted.

Really, the only place we could get hold of it was around the trunk. It would have to be grasped as if it were a bouquet of roses, as the spreading branches of the massive coral were as brittle as pipe stems.

I called for Cinderella to come down into the chamber with me, and outlined to him the unique part he was to play in my scheme. In this odd business, odd measures must be resorted to. From the photosphere window Cinderella was able to look out and observe the coral, and listening intently, he grasped what it was that I wanted him to do. Then I sent his compact ebony bulk hustling back to the surface, and waited.

Presently into my field of vision outside there came striding a grotesque black hobgoblin. It was Cinderella. Not only was he dolled up in his bubbling diving-helmet, but his legs were adorned in high rubber boots, his own idea, for protection against the stinging corals. While I measured and sketched inside the chamber, Cinderella was able to give me the relative height and spread of the tree. I was using him as a human yard-stick. When he held his arms as instructed, I got the slope of the branches.

My plan was to construct a heavy wooden cradle around the base of the coral. Would we be able to break the tree away from its stony base? We could but try it. Just then I noticed two holes in the reef

"I had been making plans for lifting the huge coral trees"
A DIVER IN THE SHADE OF AN OVERHANGING PALMATE

directly beneath the tree itself. Here was a stroke of luck! By exploding a light charge of dynamite in these openings and at the same time putting a lifting strain on the cradle, I figured I could not only dislodge the tree but obtain a slab of rock attached to it as well. The slab of bed rock would serve as a base for the specimen when it was boxed. I had Cinderella probe the depths of these holes with a pole, and, having made all necessary sketches I took my men and hurried ashore in a motor-boat.

On the hard coral beach at the Rose Island base I had a conference with my old reliable crew of blacks near the very spot where they had so recently sat upon me. With sketches and notes in hand I drew in the sand a life-sized picture of the lop-sided coral tree we had just left at the sea bottom, together with the cradle about the tree I wanted constructed. They understood what I wanted and why.

To say that these men were jacks-of-all-trades would be slighting them. They were "aces." When I passed out hammers, saws, maules and spikes, and indicated the waiting piles of lumber, my men were carpenters, and good ones, skilled especially in the tricky work in which I had trained them for years. In an hour or so the huge contraption, that was to cradle the coral tree, was built. Then came the work of padding it with sponge clipping packed into sacks and lashed securely to the cradle. When it was ready for launching, these sacks provided a nice soft fender for our coral specimen, protecting the trunk and the stout lower branches where I dared to hope for support.

No bottle was broken in the launching ceremony, though a bottle might have helped, judging from the chorus of grunts and snorts from my straining and sweating crew. To rock this cradle from the sand to the sea was no easy matter. It was made out of heavy native pine, tremendously strong, with timbers some eighteen feet long projecting far beyond the cradle proper. To these outstretching arms we would attach our lifting tackle when the wooden form was closed around the tree. No gear would touch the fragile coral branches.

A few more groans and suddenly the men lifted their burden clear of the sand and carried it into the sea. The next step was to get it out on the location and sub-merged. This was done in good tugboat fashion, and soon we were piling on sandbags and old chains, and our undersea cradle sank beneath the waves.

Imagine the thoughts of the fish world below as this massive object came into view, and tumbling after it Ward and Cinderella, a pair of bubble-throwing creatures who landed on the bottom and went into action. As a matter of precaution they first chased away a big ugly rockfish who lived in the tree, along with a flock of black angelfish. Then they closed the cradle securely about the base of the coral, dancing with

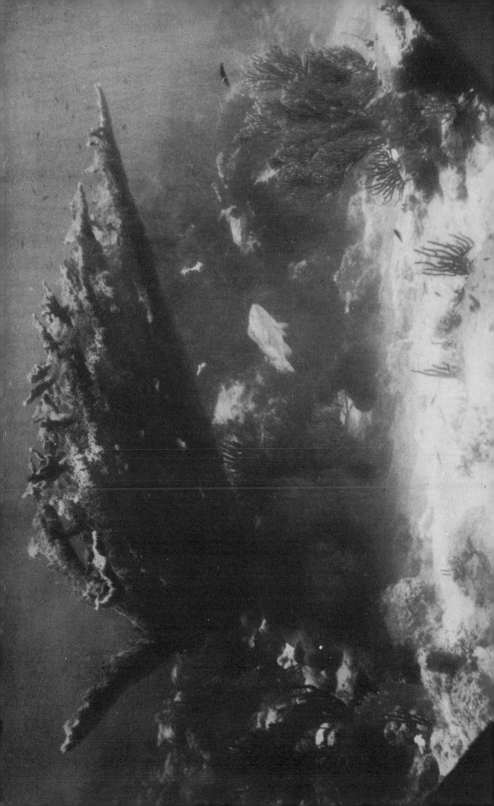

excitement when they found that it fitted like a glove. We were watching them with water glasses from the pontoons just above, and now we sent down the heavy cables and chains for the divers to fasten to each long stout arm of the cradle.

With a grinding of gears the hoisting started, but instead of the tree beginning to move up, the massive pontoons were drawn deeper and deeper down into the water. With each lift of an occasional swell we hoped that the coral would break off and land in our trap, but it would not budge even when the pontoons were drawn down until the decks were awash. The strain was terrific, but after a full hour of struggle, we were still with decks awash and the coral hadn't moved an inch. And to add to the discomfort, heavy clouds were piling up. There was every indication that a tropical squall was in store for us. No one could tell just what those clouds portended. If it was only rain, it didn't matter, but if a blow was in the squall, we were sunk.

Then down came the deluge. At last I determined to use the dynamite though I had questioned the use of it up to now. No one could be certain just how the fragile coral would be affected by the concussion from the explosion. The charges I had prepared were minute, each no larger than the end of my thumb. I sent the diver down with these tiny cartridges and instructed him to insert them in the crevices under the ledge. This done, I threw over the switch, and instantly the

293

"A more gorgeous creation was spread out before me"
GOLDEN YELLOW PALMATE CORAL TREE

pontoons rose like monsters from the sea. There had been no shock at the surface, but our coral was free. That was sure. Swinging away from the tangle of reefs, we scudded with the squall toward the shore. Thoroughly drenched with a cold pin-shower of rain, we steadily hoisted our precious load up toward the surface. We could hardly wait to see it, but at last it was revealed—not the magnificent specimen we had hoped for, but merely a shattered mass—a pile of broken branches of the twelve-foot spread of beauty we had struggled so hard to wrest from the mighty deep.

Standing on the pontoons with my now dejected crew looking not unlike so many drowned rats, there was just one man I wanted to question, but I didn't. That was the stammering, stuttering diver who had placed the explosives. I knew he had gone down alone into those eerie depths as jumpy as a darky in a grave-yard at midnight. But whether he had put the dynamite in the tree or under the tree did not matter now. There were other stone trees in our undersea quarry.

The bright sun was shining again and within an hour we were back in the glade, with the pontoons moored over another great specimen, and the *Jules Verne* close by, for I had made up my mind to be on the bottom and personally supervise the ceremonies of lifting this tree.

Scrambling down into the tube, I moved in closer and, to my delight, a more gorgeous creation was spread out before me than the one we had just blown up. Gnarled and twisted like a wind-blasted pine on a mountainside, this coral masterpiece clung to the base and side of the reef, the spread of its branches fully thirteen feet across. To add to its oddities, a family of big Nassau groupers lived under it. This tree was their castle, and from the looks of the fish as they rolled their big eyes at me as I sat busily making records, I could see that they were ready to fight to defend it, if necessary. Flashing on a pattern of stripes like a tiger one big grouper advanced toward me. In an instant he was changed, the stripes were gone and the whole body was as colourless as the white floor of the ocean. He must have been the grandfather of the lot for he turned and chased back the rest of the family, and looking very human about it, came back to give me some very dirty looks. But something more was to ruffle his serenity. Cinderella arrived in his seven-league boots. This was too much for the grouper. He dashed into a hole in the reef and turned almost black in the shadows, invisible except for a pair of red eyes that pierced the darkness.

No cradle was needed for this tree-lifting job. We could grab hold of this one through the top of its branches. Catching my signals, Ward and Cinderella were carefully guiding the one great rope-sling to the point I had estimated as the centre of gravity. Ward was on top of the tree and Cinderella under it—strange

looking figures in the setting—the sling was made fast, and I flashed the sign to go ahead with the hauling. This was the big moment. Would our plan succeed?

Powdery puffs in the sea-bed showed that the roots were giving away. The tree started upward. Cinderella rushed under to steady it. This was too much for the red-eyed grouper. We were carrying off his house and grounds. This meant fight.

Circling about the trunk of the tree, he took a bite at Cinderella and was so pleased with himself that he forgot to turn off his dark colours. The last I saw of him—just before I dashed up the tube to the surface— he was still dark and ugly, ploughing through a cloud of white fluid dust, probably rounding up his family to start out and look for a new home.

Up from the depths, my arrival on deck was greeted with war whoops that seemed to be coming from a band of wild Indians. All over the pontoons my dusky crew were doing a dance. The reason was evident. Hauled up close beneath the pontoon was the great coral tree, and absolutely intact. Not a twig of its twisted magnificence was missing. So far so good, but it still was a long way from Chicago. To get this tree out of the sea was the next problem. It weighed several tons. Soon we had towed it to the beach at Rose Island, the place I had selected to land it—if we could.

Once on the beach, no whistle was needed to remind my crew it was lunch time. After a morning of weird

297

ups and downs, I knew they were ravenous, and they wreaked their vengeance on cans of bully beef and other delicacies. At times I thought they would devour corned beef, cans and all. Loaves of bread vanished like snowflakes. No time was wasted. Finally they slowed down, took a long breath, and awaited the serving of their amber brew. These men were true Britishers, born under the flag, and addicted to the stimulating effects of tea. Their cup of hot tea was vital to their well-being and happiness.

And now for dessert I passed around saws and hammers, and they all became carpenters. What we were making we hoped later to be the bottom of the huge packing-case that would carry our big coral tree to its new home in the Field Museum. Our specimen was still suspended—not in mid-air but mid-water— just below the pontoons, but with gentle urging we soon got the wobbling tree on our immense landing platform and started the movement to pull it ashore. What could we tie to for support? Up on the sandy bluff were little palmetto-trees. They didn't mean a thing to us. There was nothing to fasten to, so hastily we dug into the hillside and located a mass of rock for our blocks and tackle. Then came the real tug-of-war.

Up to this point it had been possible to drag the huge platform, loaded with coral, over the hard sand bottom of the bay, but now as we neared the shoreline, with the weight increasing as the coral emerged from the water, we found we could not move it until we laid tracks and put rollers under the timbers of the platform. The men worked like demons. Inch by inch, foot by foot, the truly magnificent specimen rose higher and higher above the level of the sea. First at the tips, and then for the entire length of the branches, the coral turned white. The swarm of polyps were leaving it. The sea was as smooth as a millpond and I was inwardly praying that the calm would hold. A sudden squall and a tumble of waves would play havoc with our prize that now wobbled uncertainly as though it would topple over from our platform that held it.

The tide was rising just about as rapidly as our specimen was emerging from the sea, so despite our frantic efforts we seemed to gain nothing. To add to my concern, the thing I dreaded was slowly happening. A breeze had sprung up. The wind was rapidly increasing and each succeeding wave threatened to topple our three-ton tree from its resting-place, smashing the branches and ending our weary day with disaster.

Something would have to be done and done quickly if the coral were to be preserved intact. That something, I decided, was to lift the tree from its platform, level and repair its uneven base and fix it back in place, immovable. Dropping the lines, the men rushed to do my bidding, raising shears of twenty-five foot booms after bolting a crossbar at their tops and running guy-ropes from this to the top of the bluff.

With a four-ton chain-hoist attached to the cross-head, we lifted the coral tree and I examined its base. Immediately I saw what was the trouble. Several of the chunks of stone in the roots were loose. Quickly these were extracted and with an axe I began trimming the hard limestone roots, or what appeared to be roots. It was a risky business. At each blow the white stone branches above me vibrated with a high-pitched note that sent shivers up my spine. But at last the roots were evened off. The coral was gently lowered once more to the platform, and roughly boxed about the base. We poured in concrete, and the tree had a foundation which could be securely bolted and lashed to the timbers.

The rest was comparatively easy. Triumphantly we hauled it above high-water mark where it was to remain until the sun, air and water had removed all traces of animal matter from it.

Our experiences with the first two coral trees served us well. We landed the third great tree, the largest prize of the lot, with no great difficulty. This tree stood nearly six feet tall and measured fourteen by sixteen feet across its branches.

The worst was over. Compared to what we had been through, the rest of the work was almost child's play. Boat load after boat load was lifted from the depths and stored ashore to be cleaned and bleached, sometimes with the use of chemicals. Every specimen of

"Triumphantly we hauled it above high-watermark
THE LARGEST SPECIMEN OF CORAL EVER TAKEN FROM THE SEA

foliage and creature in Neptune's garden which we had not already captured, was garnered and brought to the beach; even quantities of sand from the sea-bed, for we had recorded its worm mounds and ripples and these too were to be reproduced. Soon there was a veritable fairyland on the beach, a strangely beautiful garden of corals, now cleansed and bleached to snowy whiteness. From dawn to dark the air was alive with the sounds of hammering and sawing, as the men worked to build the great boxes and crates for our prizes. Then suddenly I realized there must be a limit to the size of our cases as they were to travel by rail before they got to Chicago.

I was in a quandary, until I learned that the extreme width for railroad travel was nine feet ten inches. There was nothing to do with our largest coral but systematically to reduce it to freightage proportions. It seemed too bad to have to break off its branches even though they could be replaced in the manner a dentist pivots a tooth, but the operation was performed; and into its packing-case went our trimmed-down coral together with the trimmings. Our shipment was ready. Fifteen immense cases. There were no scales on the beach but I estimated the weight of our precious collection at at least twenty-five tons.

Day by day the calendar indicated the possibility of a hurricane. In fact, one had already started. It was on its way up from the Caribbean, though apparently not headed in our direction. If a hurricane should pounce upon us with our bulky cargo still on the beach, the results would be too awful to contemplate. Our whole collection would be tossed along the shore and broken into bits. Then nothing could ever put our coral together again.

There was just one practical way to get our load off the sands, and that was, to persuade the steamship company officials to send up one of their great barges with its enormous boom and crane to pick the boxes off the beach.

I knew the steamship company would hesitate to allow any of their vessels to negotiate the reef area. In the event of a real storm it would be a trap for their equipment as it had been for my fleet. Down to Nassau I rushed, and finally at their own price, they agreed to do the work.

It was a happy day for me when the huge crane appeared on the horizon and was towed in and moored alongside the Rose Island base. There was not a ripple on the sea—a perfect day for the transfer of the cases of coral—as the great boom swung out and took the first one, to land it safely on the deck of the barge. Then the wire slings were passed around the case holding our big thirteen-foot twisted coral tree, the one that had given us so much trouble to land through the surf, with its crumbling base. I watched anxiously the transfer of this tremendously large case, saw it go high in the air, then the boom swung over the deck of the barge and the box began to descend. But I didn't like the casual manner of the man at the controls. I wondered if he realized he was handling three tons of something as breakable as priceless cut glass. I held my breath as it started down—twenty feet from the deck—ten feet—seven feet—— Then came a whirr of the gear on the winches and a sickening thud. Down on its end bumped the box on the deck. I yelled. I cut loose a flow of seafaring language. It must have been awful. A moment before the whole beach as far as we could see had been carpeted with millions of land crabs migrating to the water. Now they had reversed and were scuttling away, pop-eyed and horrified, for the hills.

There was no remedy for the fall of the box. I groaned to think of the contents, perhaps now a broken and shattered mass of limestone. Finally I made my way out to the deck of the barge and forced myself to look into the broken end of the case, and believe it or not, a miracle had happened—not a branch of the tree had been broken. Our gloom was now changed to a scene of happiness. The saving of the tree had no doubt been the reward for our careful packing, and the method of securing this fragile specimen.

Thereafter each one of our fifteen big cases was handled as though it were filled with good fresh eggs. They were soon aboard, and off through the reefs to Nassau for transfer to the little freight steamer, *Bahamian*, which would take our coral cargo on the next leg of its journey to Jacksonville, Florida.

That trip across the gulf was the last long stretch I had left to worry about. After that our specimens might be wrecked, but not sunk.

At daybreak we started with the loading of the *Bahamian*. Dozens of crates and small cases were to go from the laboratory and elsewhere, in addition to the huge cases to be handled by the barge and crane. Then came the matter of securing the lot to prevent them from shifting with the roll of the vessel. Never was any shipment more carefully secured than this one. We hoped for the best but prepared for the worst.

It was noon before I was satisfied that all was well. The boat was to sail within an hour. But when I dashed up to the office of the U.S. consul with my invoices and bills of lading, I found that I was up against a stone wall. It was a public half-holiday and religiously observed in these balmy Bahamas. The consul himself was absent and his aide refused to attach the signature and seal of the government for free entry, although the contents of each box was fully enumerated and set forth, and its scientific purpose and destination well known even to the extent of an official letter from a director of the Field Museum to the consul himself, which I had personally delivered. This particular vice-consul now took exception to it all and began to question the commercial value of coral in general and sea-fans in particular. Sea-fans could be sold in the United States, he said. The steamer's whistle was now blowing. From the consul's window I could see the black smoke, rolling from its funnels along the water front just a block away. Then came a complaint about the form in which my papers were drawn up. They would have to be changed. I was willing to do anything to satisfy him, and dashed out to hail a carriage or some moving vehicle. It was a holiday. The streets were quiet and empty. Then thundering up the street came a rickety old truck which I stopped, and jumped into the front seat with the driver. I told him to drive, and he took me at my word, burning up the road along Bay Street to the laboratory. Pray had sailed some days before, but my wife was there and she helped me to re-type the papers. Back to the consul's office I took them, but my Nemesis still found fault.

The steamer was blowing again, and I was about to blow up myself and let it sail without the papers, when I thought of something else. Here were the wet Bahamas. There was the dry U.S.A. Any shipment headed from here to Uncle Sam was under suspicion. What more delightful trick could be played than to ship a whole boatload of wet goods marked "Coral Specimens, Handle with Care." To let the ship go without those proper papers would be not only to risk disaster but to ask for it. Should the *Bahamian* be

boarded for inspection on the high seas, I could see those revenue officers with their trusty axes at work on my cases, crashing through the corals while looking for hidden contraband. If disappointed in one case they would look for it in another, then another. After they had finished they might get satisfaction, but the museum would not.

So I rushed out to find the owner of the vessel, a man of prominence in the city, and persuaded him to come with me to the consul's office and add his oath to mine that everything was in order. He gladly did so, and pled my case with all his eloquence, but that only seemed to make matters worse. Finally I set out on the trail of the consul himself. I found him, and only then were all objections overruled. I got my papers, and finally thrust them into the hands of the good-natured captain of the *Bahamian* who had waited four hours to get them. Never was I more relieved than when I stood on the dock and saw the steamer move out.

But even then my relief was mingled with a memory of a weak link in my chain. The cargo of treasures was not insured. I had made valiant efforts to cover it adequately. Local agents were willing enough to write a policy but investigation revealed that the little steamer, which had been a crack yacht in England when Queen Victoria was young, had no rating whatsoever at Lloyds'. No company would risk a shilling that its cargo would ever land.

308

With this thought in mind, I saw the *Bahamian* steam out of the harbour and into the open sea.

That night the wind whistled an unpleasant tune, soughing through the palm-trees and whining through the screening of the laboratory living-quarters. Before retiring I had checked time and charts and knew the little *Bahamian* would soon be entering the reaches of the Gulf Stream. But sleep was fitful, and responding to my troubled dreams, twice I jumped out of bed yelling orders to my crew about reefs, ropes and riggings. I began to realize that my nerves were wound up too tight. My self-appointed task of delivering the goods according to schedule had put me on edge and there was just one place to go where rest was sure, and that's just where I was going.

With the bright sunrise next morning I was up with my new plan of action, not only for myself but for my family and my crew. We were going on a picnic— a picnic under the sea. There was plenty of time for this submarine excursion before the steamer would come to take us all back to New York.

So we answered the call of the sea, packed up our lunch, so to speak, which amounted to a truck-load of supplies, and soon the caressing influence of the deep had enfolded us. We were sailing under sealed orders or no orders at all, for I had set out to drift and go nowhere in particular. It was delightful to know that we could actually do this very thing, and rest in a

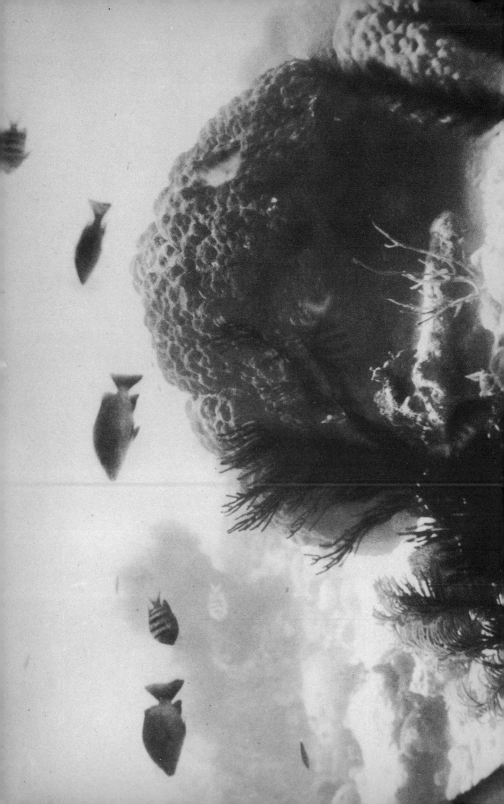

world of liquid loveliness. Sometimes the *Jules Verne* above was at anchor, but most of the time we were simply cruising along through the hills and valleys, over submarine meadows, through shadowed woods, sometimes in moonlight, only to emerge again in the lovely gardens of the sea.

In our well-ventilated studio we were as comfortable as the fish seemed to be outside our window. Of course, we were dry in our cosy chamber, breathing the normal air from above, as it rushed down our ventilator and circulated freely. Outside was water-pressure, crushing and menacing. Fathoms of ocean reached up above us, but inside the pressure was normal, the same as that enjoyed on the decks above by my native crew, now laughing and singing. I could hear them through my telephone receiver. They were on vacation. I had supplied them with everything they wanted, cartons of cigarettes, plug tobacco for their pipes, plenty of sweet stuff, including a tower of canned peaches, and also something in particular I had denied them on duty —an abundance of rock salt for salting down the fish that they captured.

My troubles had melted away. Below we were enveloped in a world of our own. I had learned to appreciate the absolute privacy of my undersea studio on my honeymoon. Now I could further enjoy it with my increasing undersea family, for now, in addition to my wife and baby, we had the youngster's pet cat.

311

"As comfortable as the fish seemed to be outside our window"
A CORAL HEAD, WAVING SEA-PLUMES AND PURPLE GORGONIAS

The deep-sea kitten was purring, delightfully content. The "Captain's" flaxen head bobbed about in the great studio window where she held forth on her big soft pillow; my wife was leisurely sketching and, as usual, I was occasionally responding to the urge to photograph. My camera was catmint to the kitten and equally fascinating to the baby. Fingers and paws were constantly poking into its lens and fittings. My focus and diaphragm adjustment meant nothing to them. However, this was everybody's picnic, and even the fish outside seemed to put on an extra effort to give us a show.

We proceeded slowly, watching the fun in the fishy arena. Digging for worms was a popular pastime. There was a radiant turbot standing on his head with his tail straight up and whirling his fins like propellers, rooting into the sandy bottom. A hog-fish ploughed with his swine-like snout, blowing up the domestic happiness of wormland in the mud. Hundreds of goat-fish grazed peacefully near, busily digging for worms. Two long white feelers adorn the chin of the goatfish, and with these he probes quickly and often. When a "strike" or the prospect of one is touched by his probe he digs in frantically to get his worm—and from the satisfied expression that invariably follows, he always gets his meal.

And right under our window, picking a course between starfish and sea cucumbers, came the mighty

"Watching the fun in the fishy arena"
GOLDEN GRUNTS AND YELLOW-TAILED GOATFISH

King-conch and the members of his family. Here my wife dropped her brushes and palette to remark, "Here come the elephants." And sure enough they did appear like a parade of pachyderms, halting and clumsy. With a ponderous importance they picked their way over the white marl sea-floor. Dancing along in the column of conchs came a frisky lieutenant, but he couldn't fool us, not from our sea-floor view. It was the shell of a conch, but it housed an invading soldier-crab. Thousands of true conchs swarmed over the sea-bed around us. As food they rate high with the natives of the islands. Cameos are cut from the lips of their shells, and sometimes they bear precious pink pearls. There are benefits and beauty in this shell-fish, so homely to look upon as it roams on the bed of the sea.

Presently we found ourselves in a darkened valley of the sea, with a shapeless bulk looming in the distance. Cautiously we drew nearer, then I realized what it was —a wreck!

Here was real adventure! To find the forgotten hulk of a long-lost ship in its watery grave! Now it bore little resemblance to its original fabric of wood and metal. Years beneath the sea had transformed it, coated it with lime, inches thick, and coral had started to grow along its ancient timbers.

In this setting of grim tragedy, everything was sombre, bathed in a deep green light, though the wreck was a haven for millions of fish that lived in and about it.

Slowly we drew near, wide-eyed with interest. Among the scintillating myriads of fish suddenly appeared a dozen big mackerel with their long lean jaws, trim bodies and bold cruel eyes. They were rounding up a great school of fish, driving them in herds with a peculiar movement until the whole mass seemed to be tied up into a knot. Then like flashing javelins the mackerel hurled themselves into the mad confusion, snapping right and left and gulping down their prey.

Scarcely was this tragedy over when a company of big horse-eye jacks made their appearance on the scene, seeming more intent upon investigating us than in gorging themselves. Heading straight for our big studio window, they looked inquiringly in, opening and closing their mouths the while as though talking about us. Then yawning and looking extremely bored, they turned and moved off in single file.

Scarcely had the gossiping jacks gone their way, when out of the mysterious depths of the wreck an immense fish cruised forth. Like an ogre from a fairy tale emerging from his dismal castle, this ugly denizen of the deep turned and made straight for our window. Closer and closer came the prognathous bulk with queer staring eyes. It was the largest jewfish I have ever seen, and as big as a shark. Slowly its great mouth opened like a yawning chasm. And for once the young "Captain" drew back into the arms of her mother who smiled at this menace outside that could not harm the little

explorer. The ogre had no designs on us and soon his hypnotic eyes were fixed on a school of fish that huddled together a few yards distant. Sidling up beside them the jewfish singled out one for his victim. Slowly under the power of the mesmeric glare this one fish swung out from the group and moved about nervously, the ogling monster following its fleeting movements. Then the huge mouth opened and the victim passed into the awaiting chasm with no more concern than a person entering a subway. This performance was repeated until apparently the correct quota had passed the turnstiles; then, blinking his eyes and barely moving his ponderous tail, the lazy old jewfish sailed back into the shadows of the wreck.

After a few more days of happy lazing of this sort my mind was relieved by a cable from Mr. Stanley Field, who had wired from Chicago that the entire collection, requiring two freight cars and a box car to carry it over the railway, had reached the museum in safety, and, I might add, within the budget.

My cares of the expedition were over. Back we hustled to the harbour at Nassau where the *Jules Verne* was anchored securely. The pontoons and the smaller craft were all hauled ashore. The equipment and undersea chamber were cleaned, oiled and stored away. The laboratory was closed, and with my family, I bade farewell to the Bahamas for a time as we boarded the steamer and headed for New York.

THE AUTHOR WITH HIS NATIVE DIVERS—
WARD, JOE, BROWN, SKIN, JAMAICA AND CINDERELLA

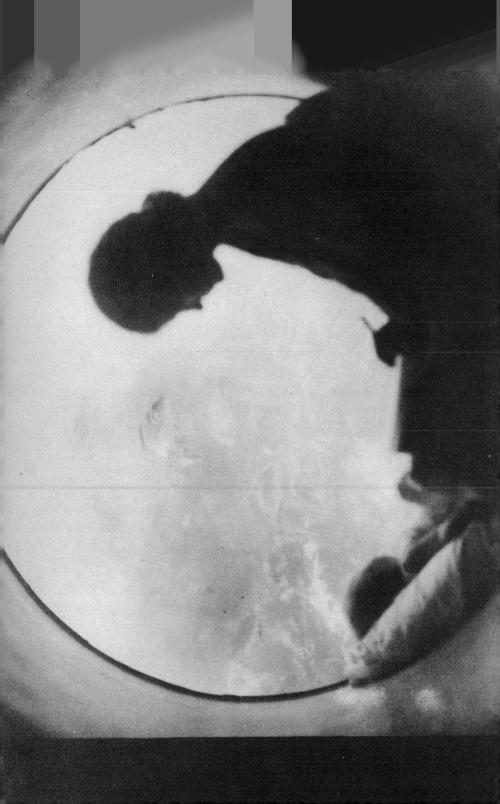

Again I caught that peculiar, intangible something in the atmosphere, and the leaden menace of the clouds that spoke of a hurricane as we reached the open sea. With no wind in particular, we encountered heavy seas all that day and the next. The third day through the wireless we heard that the hurricane had veered and was closing in on the section of the Bahamas we had just left. Wireless reports were meagre, but when we arrived in New York a full account of the disaster reached us.

The storm had struck. A seething blast had swept the reefs and islands upon which we had worked. Never in its history had Nassau experienced such a hurricane. Scarcely a building escaped serious damage from the fury of the storm. The government house was unroofed and partially destroyed. The living-quarters above our laboratory were blown completely away. Twenty dead were counted in the vicinity of Nassau. There were sixty hours of terrible suspense as the storm passed once, made a hairpin curve and returned with renewed fury.

The little freight steamer, the *Bahamian*, that had successfully carried our corals was lost for four days in the gale that tossed it about like a cork. And a similar ship which had served us all the summer, carrying our mail and supplies to and from Florida, went down in the hurricane, a total loss.

Nassau has had no hurricane since that final blast which came as the end of a cycle of storms.

319

The fates had decreed that we should miss the last of the hurricanes. We were back on bustling Broadway again, back to our routine of hotel life. It all seemed unreal, the Bahamas a million miles away. I could order a *Filet de sole* with little chance of getting a *Filet de ray*. It was a change to look out of our window into a sea of faces that were not those of fish, even though the swarm of humanity occupying the towering buildings about us reminded me of the activity of the coral polyps and their creations.

We were caught up happily in the life of the city. Yet the thrill of the great silence of the deep and the whispered song of the siren were ever luring us back to our happy hunting-ground—the world of treasures at the bottom of the sea.